A guide to Business Principles and Practices for Interior Designers

A guide to Business Principles and Practices for Interior Designers

With actual examples of the specialized procedural forms to be used in the office

by Harry Siegel, C. P. A.

Whitney Library of Design
New York

Contents

Foreword

About the Indispensable Role of Business Practice in the Highly Artistic Profession of Interior Design

The purpose of this book is to make the professional interior designer aware of basic business principles which he must heed if he is to practice his profession with reasonable monetary rewards, with the confidence of the community, and without wasting his energy or resources on business problems. In addition the book describes procedures and forms which are mandatory. It does not enter the area of the interior designer's professional qualifications such as artistic skills, creativity, or knowledge, though in analyzing business principles it refers to them.

This book is intended for interior designers in many different stages of their careers and in many different branches of the profession.

First, it is intended:
For the practicing interior designer—to show him how to analyze and solve operational problems, as well as to provide him with a multitude of essential paper forms such as letters of agreement, clients' inventory forms, billing controls, trade source forms, and budget estimate forms—which enable interior design firms to systematize and control the flow of operations, money, materials, and commitments.

This guide is also intended:
For professional interior designers employed in interior design firms or in the interior design departments of other types of firms—to give them necessary insight into operations which they may not find easy to observe clearly or wholly on the job.

For architects who maintain interior design departments in their firms in order to complete the interiors of their own buildings—as well as *for architects who specialize or hope to specialize in interior design*—to give them a clear picture of the logistics of interior design operations.

For the managers of shops, wholesale establishments, and contract firms which employ professional interior designers in order to provide their customers with design service—so that they, also, may grasp the logistics of interior design.

For the officers of corporations and institutions which maintain their own salaried staffs of interior designers to produce the interiors of their own premises—as well as *for the officers of such corporations and institutions who have occasion to engage independent interior design firms* for this work—to answer their questions on sound conduct in the field.

For the neophyte who hopes to go into practice—to outline the steps which he must take if he expects to set up an office or to associate with one—

and to describe the different forms which the firm can take, depending on the designer's needs and inclinations.

For the student—to confront him with the reality that a career in interior design means a career in business as well as in the highly esthetic art which dominates his attention during his years of professional training.

Interior design is an art. And—like all professions —it can be defined simultaneously as a profession *and* as a business. The definition and branches of the profession of interior design are covered briefly in Chapter 1, but here, in stating the purpose of this book, it is pertinent to stress the unusual importance of sound business practice in this profession. *All* professions involve business transactions, but they vary markedly in the complexity of these transactions: physicians, dentists, and lawyers pay rent, hire assistants, keep records, and send bills. But interior designers, architects, and engineers must carry through financial transactions on a very different level of complexity—and among the professions which are complex from the standpoint of business, interior design is the most misunderstood.

Partly the misunderstanding is the result of the fact that interior design has not been recognized and clearly defined as a profession for a period comparable to many of the others. Partly the misunderstanding is the direct outcome of an apparent paradox inherent in the financial transactions of the field. Often, instead of being paid like a professional person for his services, the interior designer appears to be paid like a merchant for the considerable value of material goods purchased for the interior, and it is not easy to explain that it is actually his skill in choosing and composing and handling the goods for which he is being paid. The confusion is only compounded by transactions whereby the interior designer is paid both for goods and for services—and on the basis, moreover, of systems of accounting which to the outside observer appear to be mysterious and inconsistent.

But interior design *is* complex—as an art, as a profession, *and* as a business. There is nothing wrong with that. People are complex, their lives are complex, our economy is complex, spaces are complex. What *is* wrong is that many interior designers who practice their *art* and their *profession* with undeniable competence—even with brilliant resourcefulness—fail to make a go of their careers because they do not know how to cope with their *business*. Without sound business practice, interior design is a minefield loaded with explosive charges of financial disasters, tarnished reputations, catastrophic client relations, sleepless nights.

Unfortunately few candidates for the profession are aware of these hazards. Yet the business principles which must be borne in mind to practice interior design with reasonable financial security can be grasped by any adult of competent mind. Mathematical genius is not required. With knowledge, counsel, and awareness, the designer should be able to cope with the business side of practice—without becoming obsessed or swamped by it. The first rule is to avoid venturing into the unknown territory of business without a guide. Early in his career the designer should obtain qualified business counsel.

The business fiascos which attend the careers of too many interior designers arise less from their inability to understand business principles than from their unwillingness to think seriously about business at all. They think of themselves as artists. It is fascination with line and form and color which propels them into the field as students. They are sensitive to space and proportion, mood and light. They enjoy the feel of materials—rich, rough, luscious, or fragile. They are excited by pattern. They see interiors as an expression of their clients' personalities, as solutions for psychological needs and functional requirements. They want to make people comfortable and to make difficult spaces work.

They look forward to the creation of settings which will instill flavor and drama into living—like decor for plays onstage. They love to track down *objets de vertu,* and to exploit works of art as magnets for the eye and cues to the imagination . . .

Office procedures, multiple forms, contracts, percentages? What do they care about such things?

The design schools, universities, and other educational institutions which give professional training for interior design are hard put to pack in all the courses required for purely professional and artistic competence: two and three-dimensional design; the history of architecture, interior design, and furniture; sketching, drafting, and various rendering techniques; the rudiments of architectural structure and a good command of interior architectural construction; a basic knowledge of furniture and fabric construction and a familiarity with other crafts; the basic principles of lighting design; theories of color . . . and so on and so on . . . so that by the time the three or four or five-year curriculum has been traversed, the breathless graduate is lucky if he has learned a few rudimentary facts about "the trades" and introduced himself to the people in some of the showrooms. Only a few students out of every hundred are given the opportunity for a brief pre-graduation apprenticeship in a professional firm or shop of some kind. There are more students than summer jobs, and anyhow during vacations there are too many beautiful countries to tour and too many museums to explore. Thus, having graduated with honors, having made friends and found future clients, the neophyte hasn't a notion of how to carry on an interior design practice, nor what his clients and the business community at large expect of him, nor how his operations relate to the trade sources—the industry which provides the materials and services essential to the realization of his designs. Nor—in fact—does he know how to arrive at proper fees and compensations for his services. This book brings to the attention of both the new and the practicing interior designer the business procedures of this field, so that they will have an awareness of sound and proper business conduct under the conditions that will face them in the course of professional practice.

The author has spent many years working with interior designers, solving their business problems, and developing forms and systems to reduce burdensome chores into efficient routines and clarify the control of operations. In this book he has avoided the technical jargon of accounting, finance, and legal problems, but has—in simple, direct language—presented a picture of the business operations of an interior design office from its formation through all ramifications of its dealings with clients and trade sources. In each stage he has pinpointed the problems typical of that phase, and has set forth guides to cope with them.

The author feels that he—and all designers who may find this book useful—owes a debt of gratitude to the interior designers who encouraged him to write it, and who cooperated by giving him permission to reproduce many of the paper office forms which he had developed for their practice. It was Everett Brown who first suggested that there was a need for such a book, and who encouraged him to proceed with the unaccustomed task of writing it. Melanie Kahane contributed a sizable percentage of the documents and letters reproduced in it, and gave him much needed inspiration in hurdling some of the more formidable phases of the project. Thanks for this kind of essential inspiration and help are also due to Yale R. Burge, J. H. L. Chambers Jr., Marvin K. Culbreth, Audré Fiber, Joseph Grusczak and his partner J. Ray Baker, Michael Greer, Ellen Lehman McCluskey, Daren Pierce, Rita St. Clair, and Elaine Siegel.

Authoritative advice on insurance was contributed by Matthew and Morton Kornreich. Matters pertaining to law and legal terminology were worked over and checked by Saul Sorkin. Indispensable advice on working with craftsmen and workrooms was contributed to the chapter on relationships with trade sources by William Goldfinger and William Schaffro.

And last but not least, the author wishes to express his grateful acknowledgement for the insights into the profession which he has derived from his association with the National Society of Interior Designers and the American Institute of Interior Designers, the professional organizations which have piloted the interior designers of our country into a full realization of their professional identity.

Olga Gueft

Forms illustrated in this book
are obtainable from:

Interior Designers Forms Company
Division of Murphy Printing Co., Inc.
56 Hamilton Avenue
White Plains, New York 10601

Send $1.00 For Forms Catalog (Credited
to first purchase)

Part 1 A Practice in Interior Design and How to Establish One

Chapter One

Interior Design as a Profession

Profession

"a vocation or occupation requiring advanced training in some liberal art or science, and usually involving mental rather than manual work"
—*Webster's New World Dictionary*

What we mean by the word *profession* was clearly understood by the general public long before the dictionary writers made it official. The term *interior designer,* however, was hardly in use at all until about four decades ago, and did not formally supersede the word *decorator* until the mid-fifties. At that time both of the two leading American organizations representing the profession made it part of their names. The elder, founded in 1931, acknowledged the obsolescence of the term, *decorator,* in 1961, when it changed its name from the American Institute of Decorators to the American Institute of Interior Designers (without changing its insignia initials, A.I.D.). The younger organization used the term from the outset, calling itself the National Society of Interior Designers (N.S.I.D.) since it was founded in 1957.

The history of the profession is beyond the scope of this book, but the change in terminology is significant. Throughout the recorded past, interiors had been designed and fabricated by people operating under innumerable vocational guises and with many different relationships to the patron or client on one hand and to the workmen, artisans, and suppliers on the other. Interiors have been produced by architects, builders, artists, sculptors, artist-craftsmen, artisans, upholsterers, drapers, cabinet-makers, shopkeepers, antique dealers, and, after World War I, by imaginative, magnetic amateurs high on the social scale. It was with the advent of the very last group that the term *decorator* became important and popular. It is still preferred for conversational purposes today by people who understand that it is a misleading term, because the term *interior designer* is, to be honest, a rather more awkward mouthful. But *decorator* is ambiguous; it can mean a painter or paperhanger; it can mean a housewife with spare time on her hands and all the brass but none of the talent of the late Elsie de Wolfe, Lady Mendl—the original and greatest of the society decorators. *Interior designer* means a professional, and the two organizations have defined his functions and qualifications very clearly. The following paragraphs combine, for the sake of succinctness, the very similar definitions published by both of the organizations:

Interior designers are defined as those individuals who are qualified to practice in the profession of interior design and who have completed a four-year course at the college or university level in which academic and technical training in design are combined and who have had not less than three years (N.S.I.D.) or four years (A.I.D.) of practical experience in a recognized establishment of interior design and decoration; or

who are actively engaged in the profession of interior design and have completed a course of secondary-school level and have had a minimum of two years of academic work of college level and three years of technical training in a chartered school of design, and who have had not less than four years (A.I.D.) or three years (N.S.I.D.) of full-time practical experience in a recognized establishment of interior design and decoration.

In addition to professional qualifications, professional standards and ethics are demanded of practitioners:

"The profession of Interior Design demands that its members have high standards, training, integrity, imagination and creative ability. The services of the interior designer should include any service

that shall further the ultimate goal of creating an environment of orderliness and beauty. The interior designer shall maintain his professional integrity; his motives, abilities and conduct shall always be such as to command respect and confidence."

—From the Code of Ethics of the American Institute of Interior Designers

The brief period between the popular recognition of the phenomenon known as the *decorator* and the official definition of the professional *interior designer* has been marked by the emergence of a distinct power on the American scene. Both in an economic and in an esthetic sense, the interior design profession is exerting an important, observable, and measurable influence on the American style of life. In capturing the imagination of the public, it has added much to our awareness of the surroundings of our daily lives, to our intelligent handling of the factors of comfort, convenience, efficiency, and ease in the arrangement of the places where we live and work. It has added to our enjoyment of the sensuous and artistic components of our environment, to our discrimination in appraising old and new objects of art and craftsmanship.

The emergence of the profession entails more, however, than capturing the *imagination* of the public; the national pocketbook is in tow as well, and we can go further and say that our commercial structure is involved. The profession has developed in tandem with a distinct industry—the interior furnishings industry (a more accurate term than *home* furnishings industry). The operations of the interior furnishings industry reflect the enormous demand for quality products generated by the profession. It also makes possible the efficiency with which the profession can now provide what might be called custom or personal service on a mass scale. Working with "the trades," which offer an amazing selection of products and services, the profession controls a sizable and steadily growing percentage of the discretionary expenditures of the public—both the individual public and the corporate and institutional public (including the government).

By the very definition of the word, interior designers are professionals. By the very impact of their work on society, they are professionals. By and large they conduct themselves as professionals in the esthetic and technical phases of their endeavors. But in the business and financial aspects of their work, too many of them still operate as rank amateurs. This can be disastrous, because the budgeting and control of money for the desired esthetic result is as important a part of their service as the esthetic result in itself. The very nature of the designer's service makes the financial aspect of his work complex, difficult—and essential. The designer does not usually stop at giving advice or producing drawings for interiors, but goes on to assume the responsibility for the translation of those ideas and drawings into tangible reality, becoming involved in the specifying, ordering, and installation of a huge dollar volume of goods and services. Herein lies the crucial importance of professionalism in the business aspects of interior design. It is not enough for the interior designer to achieve a professional level of competence in designing beautiful, appropriate, and functional interiors. It is also essential that he manage to achieve a professional level of competence in organizing his operation—whatever its size—in his business dealings with his clients, in his business dealings with his trade sources, in determining and collecting his fees and compensations, in running his firm both on a short and a long-term basis.

A professional group with such economic impact

needs to conduct its affairs in a rational manner, both to insure a reasonable financial return to its members, and to maintain its place in the economy.

It is pertinent here to be specific about just where it is that the profession stands in the economy. An analysis of twelve design organizations which are clients of my own accounting firm is revealing:

These firms range in size from the largest—with a staff of twelve professional designers doing a volume of one-million dollars a year in gross billings, to the smallest—with one professional doing one-hundred thousand dollars in gross volume. In one year these twelve firms billed a total of $4,-477,153. for goods, services, and fees, and purchased for their clients $3,086,942. worth of goods and services. If one accepts the fact that there are at least 12,000 design firms of unequivocally professional status in our country, it is safe to state that the U.S. interior design profession controls the flow of merchandise and services in the interior furnishings industry to an amount well in excess of four-billion dollars.

In summary, is it not mandatory to view the profession as a major part of America's business scene, and is it not mandatory to conduct its affairs in the sound, businesslike manner befitting the formal definition of a professional, and not as some wit has defined the interior designer:

"Someone who tells you what kind of furniture to buy, what kind of draperies to hang, what colors to use around your house—sort of like a mother-in-law with a license."

Chapter Two

Divisions of the Profession

The interior designer's function—to plan, design, and execute interiors of all kinds—encompasses a wide variety of services, a wide variety of business organizations offering such services, a wide variety of collaborative arrangements. Specialization is not compulsory in the profession, and there are many versatile designers or design firms which do many kinds of work; other designers may specialize in different kinds of work over a period of years. But the tendency to specialize is natural, and business conduct as well as professional activity follows well-established lines in each division of the profession.

The most important division is between residential and non-residential interior design. Though many designers do both, it is nevertheless true that specialization in one or the other implies important differences in temperament, working habits, and business conduct.

Residential interior design is for the *private* living quarters of *individuals* or individual families. We italicize the words *private* and *individuals* because strictly speaking the term *residential* is misleading. Hotels, school dormitories, and many kinds of institutions can be defined as residential, but are not included under the classification of residential interior design because the client is not the ultimate particular occupant but a commercial or institutional entrepreneur who is preparing interiors for others to occupy; also the relationship between client and designer is therefore different and less personal. In residential work much more time is usually spent by the designer in solving particular or one-of-a-kind details, and this has a decisive bearing on the economic or financial rationalization of the work.

Residential interior design may encompass a whole residence or only a part of one. It may entail all of the functions involved in creating the area involved, or only one or some. The job may entail:

A. **Planning, designing, executing and furnishing**
— a complete private house or apartment
— or only specified rooms or parts of rooms—or

B. **Consultation or technical service on**
— color coordination
— painting and wall covering schedules
— specifications for specially-built units
— consultation with craftsmen or architects
— developing layouts or floor plans
— producing renderings, other presentations, working drawings.

The personal nature of the client-designer relationship in residential work accounts for the fact that there are few hard-and-fast rules about exactly which services a designer may perform for a client. But there are certain clearly recognized tendencies, and it is therefore possible to generalize about what it takes to make a designer who will be happy and successful when specializing in residential work. It may be true that one can find interior designers specializing in residential work who produce plans, room designs, and detail specifications for a fee and stop at that point, leaving the client to do his own purchasing, but this is the *exception* to the rule. The rule is that designers in the residential field do less drawing and detailing and more purchasing of single items than designers in the non-residential field.

Under most conditions residential work does not pose insurmountable obstacles for the reasonably competent, reasonably businesslike interior designer. By reasonably competent we mean equipped with the talent and training required to design attractive and functional interiors. By reasonably businesslike we mean able to solve not only the design problems that are posed on the drawing board, but the practical problems of dealing with clients and workmen, and of finding one's way through the financial mazes of budgeting, billing, and collecting that very essential commodity called money.

Paramount among the qualifications for personal satisfaction and success in the residential field is an interest in people and an ability to deal with them. This does not imply that the personal equation is not important in non-residential work, but that it is *more* imporant in residential work. To put it crassly, for each dollar earned, more hangs on the designer's insight and tact. The designer must in each case develop rapport with the client both culturally and financially. He must put his finger on the client's real needs, on his way of living and what it requires in functional facilities and esthetic background—whether or not the client can express it adequately or is even aware of just what it is. From the standpoint of working habits, the designer must have sufficient patience and attention to detail to enable him to adhere meticulously to the realities of the client's budget. And as far as his professional equipment is concerned, thorough familiarity with market sources is primary—familiarity with lines *and* prices (at least in general)— because residential work involves so many relatively small purchases (of single items or small quantities) that inefficiency in research-type shopping can be detrimental to the profit picture.

If each residential job is to be a success from the client's point of view, profitable from the designer's, and an enhancement to his reputation as well, normal orderliness in following the sequence of working procedures is essential. First careful interviewing to establish the client's program and budget, then development of a design concept, then obtaining the client's approval of that concept, then making estimates, then making authorized purchases, then supervising and installing. A designer cannot rely completely on his esthetic performance, for success also depends upon a firm understanding of the procedures needed to translate the concept into an interior well done and satisfactory financially as well as emotionally.

The designer also must be fore-armed with a realistic awareness of his own shortcomings or gaps in his technical know-how. If any job calls for more than his grasp of electrical planning, air-conditioning, or architectural structure, he had better rely upon qualified architects, engineers, general contractors, and so on. And he had better know how to collaborate with them. It is sound practice to establish steady working relationships with experts and technicians who are likely to be needed on a long-term basis in the course of a career. It is impossible to be all things to all people; an attempt to do so can only lead to disaster.

Non-residential work includes all areas of concern to the business world, institutions, and government —hotels, motels, offices, banks, retail establishments large and small, schools, hospitals, other custodial institutions, showrooms, factories, museums, galleries, theaters, movies, restaurants, beauty parlors, gymnasiums, night clubs, discotheques, bowling alleys, and so on. In the field Non-Residential work is sometimes loosely called Contract work, implying a more formalized and precise business relationship between client and designer and a different purchasing procedure for the characteristically larger quantities of goods and services involved.

Non-residential work is becoming more important every year because the business community has come to accept the crucial importance of good professional interior design in determining the success

17

of commercial enterprises. The client is not, as in residential work, the only person to be satisfied. The designer has also to consider the client's client —or his customer, his employees, and the public in general. Success and failure are measured in the comings and goings of masses of people over a period of time; in the efficient or inefficient use of costly space; in efficient or inefficient circulation patterns that in turn affect the use of costly employee-hours; in the ability of employers to attract and hold competent employees essential to their operations; in the replacement cycle of furnishings.

The client in non-residential work is a business man or businessmen—we speak of the corporate client—or the board of trustees of an institution. The corporate client expects sound business thinking and sound business methods from the interior designer. While a sound business approach ought to characterize residential as well as non-residential work, it is an absolute must in non-residential work.

Even to get the commission in non-residential work, the designer must project the image of a responsible business organization. The selling approach must be highly organized long before the design concept is formulated. Either the client or the client's management consultant, or the architect or the interior designer must analyze the logistics of the client's operation in the premises to be designed; space planning may be a necessary prelude to the development of a design concept. (This is not to imply that a firm should invest time in planning research unless the client agrees to compensate for research time whether or not the design firm gets the commission—a stricture which applies to all major time investments made in hopes of winning a commission. Chapter 17 on Client Contacts in Non-Residential work covers

this point more fully.)

The design firm in non-residential work must be organized to proceed in logical steps somewhat more elaborate than in the residential field: from the preparation of rough layouts to the coordination of information into architectural drawings; to construction specifications, electrical and ventilation requirements; working drawings; specifications for suppliers of materials; and finally coordinating the work of the various trades and the installation.

To accomplish all this and deal rationally with his clients, sources, and workmen, the designer must have a well-organized office capable of solving design problems, expediting technical coordination, and carrying the load of paper work needed to control each step of the operation. Last but not least, the designer must be sophisticated in balancing the financial factors of fees and costs which will determine the profits of the operation.

Interior Design Service in Retail Establishments.
Many interior designers operate retail shops in which the retail operation may equal or surpass design service as a source of income. Often but not always, the owner-designer provides design service without charge while selling merchandise at retail, receiving his compensation in the form of the normal profit. This type of enterprise calls for fairly ample capital to establish the business and maintain working inventory. The two phases of the operation tend to complement each other helpfully. The availability of attractively displayed merchandise attracts customers, and the availability of competent design service solves any problems which might cause them to hesitate or make mistakes expensive to themselves or—if the shop makes an exchange in such a case—to the shop. The rapid growth of interior design departments in large de-

partment and homefurnishings stores testifies to the effectiveness of this kind of operation. So does the proliferation of office furniture dealerships which offer service in office design and space planning.

Product Design by Interior Designers.
The scholastic route to a diploma in interior design overlaps the scholastic route to a diploma in related design fields—including industrial and graphic design, not to mention the fine arts. Most interior design students are taught how to design fabrics, and how to construct furniture. Many interior designers design custom furniture, fabrics, and accessories for particular interiors. It is very natural for them to design original lines of furniture, fabrics, accessories, lamps, and other objects for manufacture. And it is not at all surprising that some of the most influential items on sale in the interior furnishings market are the product of interior designers rather than of specialists in furniture design or whatever field was involved. In such work interior designers have the real advantage of knowing what is needed and what will work, and certainly they have a more natural affinity for interior furnishings than industrial or product designers. For in industrial design the emphasis is on solving production problems for machine manufacture—a factor which is of minor importance in the interiors field.

Association in Architectural, Engineering, and Other Firms.
The new awareness of the importance of professionally designed interiors has had a noticeable effect on the practice of architecture. Many architects are eager to contract for the interiors of the buildings they design if these are owner-occupied. It is noticeable that many of the most prestigious of our architectural firms—the Skidmore, Owings & Merrills and Welton Beckets—who had small or no interior departments ten or twenty years ago have large ones today. A few interior departments within architectural offices have a degree of autonomy, taking on interior commissions in collaboration with architectural firms other than their own. Interior Space Design, the interior division of the architectural-engineering firm of Perkins & Will, is the best known of this type; its offices are not only in a different location, but in a different city from that of the parent firm.

Thus, when it comes to bidding for interior jobs, interior design departments compete as separate entities. One observes cases where architectural firms, having bid for and failed to win the interior job on one of its own buildings, will collaborate with an independent interior design firm or even with the interior division of another architectural firm. The question of who gets the job is decided by competitive bidding on the basis both of costs and of concepts. Obviously, the interior design firm which wants to swim along with this school of well-fed fish has to be completely in command of their procedures and vocabulary. It is not at all unusual to find architects employed in interior design firms of this class. Architects have not been slow to grasp the fact that there is money to be made in interiors. To hold his own among them the interior designer must take systematic steps to learn how to:

1. Work in cooperation with architects,
2. Bid successfully in competition with architects,
3. Enhance the unique value of the interior designer's contribution in projects in which the various environmental professions work as a team.

Chapter Three

Business Formations

No designer can set himself up in practice without first setting up a business organization. It shouldn't be necessary to make such a ridiculously obvious statement, but it is. Many designers commit themselves to the dream of making beautiful interiors happen without stopping to make the decisions and to go through the formalities which must be attended to before the community will acknowledge their legal right to do business. These decisions and formalities cannot be evaded even if the designer wants to start small—as small as a one-man office. For not even the one-man office can function until a business vehicle has been provided to roll it along. Such a vehicle can take one of four basic forms—the four business formations which are the subject of this chapter. They are defined and discussed further on, after brief explanations of why choosing the right one is so important, but the categories are named:

1. The individual form company
2. The associate relationship
3. The partnership
4. The corporation

Determining which one will best serve the needs and inclinations of the particular designer is the first step in launching a practice. It is also one of the most important decisions the designer will have to make, for each of these four forms entails its own particular advantages and disadvantages relating to financing and operation. Far from being arbitrary, the choice should be calculated as rationally as possible. The design field in which the designer expects to practice (subject of the preceding chapter) should carry a great deal of weight. In addition there are legal and fiscal technicalities involved which make it advisable to get expert counsel from a Certified Public Accountant or lawyer experienced in the interiors field.

Before defining each of these four basic business formations and discussing its advantages and disadvantages for interior designers, it should be pointed out that such decisions, though important, are not necessarily final and forever. A designer's practice may grow, change character, and develop new ramifications; the climate of business in which he operates may also change. Whatever decisions he made as a beginner, the experienced designer should periodically have his original decision reviewed. It may be wise to consider a metamorphosis in the type of business formation if the practice that is being carried by this formation has altered over the years.

The interior designer's decision on the form of his business is more portentous than that of the architect or members of other professions because the interior designer has a far broader choice—a choice virtually unlimited. Lawyers, physicians, accountants, and certain other professionals, for example, are not legally free to incorporate. None of them are free—as the interior designer still is at present—to declare themselves in practice without first passing examinations and meeting other requirements for licenses. Unrestricted, the interior designer can choose any business structure he pleases, asking himself only, "What is best for me?"

1. **Individual Form**
   The simplest and least expensive business formation to organize is the *individual form* (which is the correct technical term). In this form, the company and the individual owner are one and the same entity, so that the firm has no existence apart from the owner (and cannot continue to exist after his death unless steps are taken to change the company's formation into one of the other types described in this chapter). In the individual form, the owner is both the controlling manager and the owner of

all of the company's assets. He receives all of the profits, and is personally responsible for all of the losses.

To organize in the individual form requires no formality of any kind at this writing, since licenses to practice interior design are not yet required in any state.

All that is required is:

1. Deciding the location of the firm and its commercial nature, that is, whether it will be an office, shop, home-studio, or whatever.

2. Registering with such tax offices as the community requires. For example, sales taxes are levied in some but not all states, and in some but not all cities. Since the firm is expected to collect such taxes from its customers and transmit the money to the appropriate government office, the company must be registered with that government office, acquiring an identifying "resale number".

3. Opening a bank account in the name of the firm.

4. Establishing credit and trade source relations.

5. Setting up the necessary stationery and printed forms for office use (what these forms are is shown in various subsequent chapters).

However, before deciding to organize his company in the individual form, the designer should stop to think about the following considerations:

A. *Unlimited liability and its potential dangers.*

B. *Possible income tax disadvantages.*

C. *The question of the firm name.*

A. *Unlimited liability and its potential dangers:*

The individual form of doing business does not afford the protection of limiting liabilities to the assets of the business. The owner is personally liable not only for all losses and debts but for every adverse effect of the operation. If the operation should become heavily involved in debt, creditors can proceed against personal assets owned by the designer which are not part of the regular structure of the business. If the designer is married, a judgment creditor may under certain conditions be able to reach the jointly owned assets of owner and spouse. It cannot be overemphasized that the individual form affords no protection in limiting the liabilities that could occur, except for those which may properly be covered by insurance (which liabilities are discussed in Chapter 24).

The extent and nature of the unlimited liability which may result from the operation of an individual form business should be reviewed by the designer's attorney, since these liabilities vary in different parts of the country.

B. *Income taxes and possible disadvantages therein:*

Since tax dollars are not minor in today's scheme of things, it is wise to examine the tax implications of the business formation which the designer is contemplating. If he chooses the individual form, the designer will report the net income (or loss) of his business on his individual income tax return, listing the figures under Schedule C and adding them to his other income to arrive at his net taxable income. Inasmuch as income tax rates rise on an escalating basis, the more the taxpayer reports as net taxable income, the higher the tax rate he will pay. This is of particular importance to those who have additional sources of income, be these in the form of salaries, royalties, dividends, interest, capital gains, etc. It is also significant to married designers whose spouses have incomes of their own. In some cases the tax advantages which the couple might have gained by paying their income taxes on a joint return may be counterbalanced by the high tax rate to be paid on the total income they will report when they have added the spouse's income to the profit earned by the designer's company—should he have chosen to organize his company as an individual form business. The designer should have the tax consequences analyzed in light of his personal situation, comparing the taxes he will pay if he has an individual form business with those he would pay if he were operating under a corporate structure.

C. The question of the company name:

The new designer should be alert to the impression made by the name of his firm on trade sources and potential clients. The name should imply that the designer is a firmly organized business entity. The firm's name is frequently the first tangible thing with which the designer makes contact with the business world. It should make a strong impression and help the designer build an image of stability and operational know-how. The name of a private individual, which is the most likely and natural name for an individual form company, can imply a lack of organizational power and financial stability, with a dampening effect on credit applications in the trade as well as on potential clients, particularly corporate clients. The "Inc." or "Ltd." which can only be added to the name of an incorporated firm enhances its im-

pressiveness immeasurably. This is not to imply that the owner's name is the only possible name for an individual form company. Designers can and often do title their firms with assumed names—"Bon Mot Design Company"—or use their own names as the basis for an enlarged title—"Mary Jones Interiors Company". The designer who wishes to solve the name question in this way should be aware, however, that each community has its own legal requirements regarding the use of assumed names. It is important to check this requirement in each community and to register the assumed name with the proper authorities.

2. **Associate Status**

Before deciding to organize a company of his own, it may be worthwhile for the designer to consider an alternative working arrangement—to associate with an already organized company. Associate status is distinctly different from the position of an employee. Associate status offers many of the advantages of owning one's own business with very few of the disadvantages. It requires virtually no capital and risks none, but it allows the designer-associate as much freedom as the designer-owner to follow his own esthetic bent and to reap financial rewards—and full credit as well—for his own initiative, efficiency, and talent. The associate arrangement is excellent for both new and experienced designers. It gives the new designer guidance and all the facilities of a going concern. It gives the experienced one a base from which to operate without involving him in the humdrum administrative chores and details of running an office.

What it *does* require is that the designer have something to offer to the company in turn—perhaps "a following"—i.e. potential clients—or else an obvious and perhaps unusual talent or high degree of expertise in some phase of interior design in which the other associates of the firm are relatively weak.

If the owner or owners of the firm invite a designer to join, the designer arranges to bring his work to the company, though he makes no investment and does not concern himself with the administrative, financial, or personnel problems of the company. His responsibilities encompass client contact, all phases of planning and design, market research, the preparation of purchasing specifications, and supervision of the final installation. The company provides staff to perform all clerical work, actual ordering, payments to the sources, billing to the client.

Under this arrangement the designer and the company share a fixed percentage of the gross profits of each job, the gross profit being the difference between the billing price to the client and the actual prime cost of tangible items and services provided. The designer's percentage varies from 60% to 40% depending on the extent of the services rendered by the company. All normal operating and administrative expenses are paid for by the company and are not charged to the associate. The only exceptions are travel expenses, drafting, blueprints, and other cost items which are specific to each particular job.

In some instances the associate may work on jobs in which the client is not his but the company's. In such instances his split of the gross profit will be smaller than when he has brought the client in himself, usually ranging from 40% to 20%.

To the young designer the associate basis is an excellent platform from which to launch a career, since a tremendous amount of valuable know-how can be gained by working with one's own clients with the help of experienced designers and a functional business operation. It is the natural place to start for the designer who has contacts but doesn't know how to make the first formal and financial steps to develop these contacts—or if he has contacts but no capital. Subject, of course, to the operating methods and policies of the firm, the associate enjoys immeasurably greater freedom and opportunity than an employee. The mutual rewards of association can be enormous to all concerned. To the established firm it offers a means of bringing in new blood and new clients, of changing a fading image, of keeping up with changes in taste and demand.

3. **Partnership**

Webster defines partnership as: "Two or more persons engaged in the same business enterprise and sharing its profits and risks." The partnership form of doing business is a possibility for two or more designers who feel that they would make a good team, complementing and reinforcing each other in talent and experience. The idea of partnership occurs naturally where two designers have a compatible esthetic bent but different strengths in terms of the ability to attract clients, negotiate in the market, and handle various technical phases of the work. It also occurs logically where designers feel that they need to share the burden of being continuously on the alert, where they feel that being on call and on the job day in and day out, year in and year out, is beyond their endurance. Partnership offers the possibility of relief from one of the great disadvantages of the one-man (or one-principal) company—the necessity to work under pressure without respite for long periods when jobs come in thick and fast.

So two or more can share the capital risks, as well as the responsibilities, can divide their time "on duty", and exchange ideas; two brains can be better than one.

Because of its very simplicity and the obvious appeal of its advantages, the partnership form is often plunged into without sufficient consideration about its disadvantages.

The Disadvantages and Hazards of Partnership:
Responsibility for the Actions of the Partner:
The partnership firm as a whole and all of the individual partners are responsible for the actions of each and every partner. Whatever any partner does in business, whatever promises he makes to clients or to the trade, whatever papers he signs drunk or sober are binding on the firm and on each partner together and separately. Whatever damages, losses, mistakes, or lapses he may bring on by omission or commission are never the problems of the miscreant alone but of the innocent partner or partners as well.

Unlimited Liability:
As in the individual form of company, members of a partnership are personally liable for the financial effects of the business, and there is no limiting the satisfaction of these liabilities solely to the assets of the partnership. In the event of insolvency, the creditors can proceed against the assets of all or any member of the partnership—and possibly of the partners' spouses as well. Whatever losses are incurred by an irresponsible partner become, as stated in the preceding paragraph, liabilities against the other partner or partners. The point of this

paragraph is to add the extremely significant fact that these liabilities are unlimited. The personal assets of each and every partner are legally liable to attachment by creditors to redeem losses incurred without his knowledge by a person who may have been drunk, demented, or driven by malice. To repeat: the choice of a partner is no light matter. Even if all partners are scrupulous in their dealings with each other, however, and perform their work to the best of their ability, the unlimited liability feature of the partnership form of enterprise remains as a serious hazard and disadvantage, for losses can and do occur through innocent misjudgment and even through sheer bad luck. Whatever the cause of the loss, in a partnership —as in an individual form company—the designer runs the risk of losing not only the assets of the business but his shirt and possibly his wife's jewelry.

Income Tax Disadvantages:
The partnership form of business structure exposes the partners to the same possibility of income tax disadvantages as the individual form does. The tax laws regard partners as individuals, and tax the profits of a partnership as individual income. The Federal Income Tax requires that the income which each partner earns as his share of the profits of the partnership be added to his "other source of income" in his personal return, raising the total taxable income to a higher possible figure and subjecting that figure to an escalated tax rate—in other words to the higher possible tax rate. As in the case of the individual form company, the designer contemplating the organization of a partnership should have a competent business counsellor estimate the personal income taxes he would have to pay for a given income with the taxes he would pay under the possibly lower

corporation rates that would apply if he organized his company as a corporation instead.

Simple as the partnership form is, it nevertheless requires the formation of a business vehicle, and there are definite formalities involved which entail the service of an attorney. Competent legal counsel will cover all facets of a properly drawn agreement and also conform the new enterprise to existing local legal requirements and necessary registrations. It is imperative to understand that the partnership form of doing business should not be entered into without this partnership agreement. Among the pertinent factors which the partners must decide and include in the legal agreement are:

1. Capital contributions
2. Share of the profits
3. Use of drawing accounts
4. Definition of responsibilities
5. Methods of dissolving the partnership in the event of

    a. Mutual agreement to dissolve
    b. Retirements
    c. Death

Before deciding to draw up a partnership agreement, the parties involved should consider the following questions:

1. Do you know and understand your future partner?
2. Can you mesh as personalities under the pressures of work over a long period?
3. Will each partner carry a fair share of the burdens of management and work?
4. Will each partner bring in a fair share of business?
5. Are the partners reasonably similar in esthetic bent and general level of professional proficiency?

6. Have you thoroughly studied the disadvantages and hazards of partnership?

4. The Corporate Form of Doing Business

It has probably not escaped the reader that in discussing certain disadvantages of the individual form and the partnership forms of doing business, I have suggested that the corporate form may offer relative freedom from these disadvantages, and that it should be seriously considered by a designer (or designers) who intend to go into practice. Even before defining it, it is important to point out that almost everywhere the corporate form *is* a possible alternative to the individual form and the partnership.

By definition a corporation is "an association of individuals, created by law, having a continuous existence independent of its members, and powers and liabilities distinct from those of its members." But remember, you can legally have a corporation consisting of only *one* individual (in most states) or a corporation of *two* (or of course more) individuals. What counts is not the number of people who own a corporation but the fact that the corporation is a *separate entity;* legally and financially it exists apart from its owners. Herein lie the all-important differences between an individual form company or partnership and a corporation.

Organizing a corporation entails legal formalities. An attorney must be retained, since the procedures, and the structure of the corporation must conform with the laws of the state in which the company is incorporated.

Advantages of the Corporate Form:
1. Limited Liability.
The most important advantage of the corporate

25

form is that it limits the liability of the stockholder to the amount invested by him, and, generally speaking, the stockholder is not personally liable for financial losses resulting from the operations of the business beyond—again—the sum invested by him (except to the government in regard to certain taxes). However great the company's debts, creditors cannot, generally speaking, go beyond the assets of the corporation because the corporation and the owners of the shares of stock are *not* one and the same entity. The debts of the corporation are *not* the debts of the designer.

From this viewpoint the corporate form is exceptionally well suited to the interior design field. In viewing the business form to select, the designer must realize that this kind of work involves not only the usual risks of debt which threaten business enterprises of every description, but also a higher degree of risk which arises in the handling of a client's funds, the handling of a client's own goods, and the purchasing, processing, and transportation of goods from trade sources.

2. *Income Tax Benefits.*
Income tax laws treat the corporation as a separate entity subject to its own tax rates. In many cases the effective corporation tax rate that applies may be appreciably lower than the rate that would apply if the company's profits were included in the owner's individual tax return.

At the present time (1967-1968) the base corporate tax rate is 22% on net income up to $25,000. Therefore, if an individual is in a personal income tax bracket above 22%, he can, to an extent, shelter the income from his design firm by operating it as a corporation, subjecting its profits to a flat 22%—instead of the effective tax rate which would be assessed against the income if he were operating his firm as an individual form company.

In any case a competent professional tax accountant should be consulted to analyze the comparative tax picture of the firm as a corporation versus another business structure.

Current tax regulations have eased somewhat the problem of surplus accumulation and the mandate to declare dividends—which in the case of small businesses may sometimes create burdens counterbalancing the tax advantage of the corporate form. Such burdens are now eased to the extent that a corporation is permitted to accumulate up to $100,000 in surplus before declaring dividends—avoiding a double tax on dividends and profits.

The designer's tax counsellor should also investigate another tax innovation: the use of Subchapter S Corporation allows the profits or losses of the corporation to be taxed at personal income tax rates, while still retaining the corporate structure and the corporate advantage of limited liability. This can be an advantageous ploy for young firms that may possibly suffer losses in the first years of business operation.

2. *Issuance of Stock for Capital.*
If the firm needs additional capital, corporation law allows the managers to attract investment money by issuing and selling shares of stock.

3. *Immortality.*
The corporation's identity and activity are unaffected by the death or disability of any or all stockholders.

*4. Superior Profit-Sharing and
   Pension Benefits.*

The benefits from profit-sharing and pension plans which can be derived under corporation regulations are significantly superior to those allowed in individual form companies or partnerships. This is another obvious avenue of investigation for the designer's financial counsellor.

In summarizing the corporate form as a possibility for the designer who wants to create a business vehicle for his practice, it is the advantage of limited liability which should be stressed as the overriding consideration. The operations of a design practice incur liabilities even in a corporation, but the creditors (except certain preferred creditors in a few very special cases) cannot seek reimbursement from the personal assets of the individual stockholders. And since the ordering of goods, the handling of the client's funds, and the processing of the client's own goods create never-ending opportunities for high damages and losses . . . and since interior designers are apt to pay more attention to esthetic than to business problems . . . they should avail themselves of any umbrella which offers protection from the hazards of operating in their chosen field. The corporate organization form is one of the biggest and best umbrellas available to them.

The disadvantages of the corporate form lie in the formal technicalities and costs of incorporating, prescribed formalities to be followed during the existence of the corporation, and certain state franchise and stock taxes.

Chapter Four

Location and Nature of the Business

Having decided which business formation to choose for his practice, and in what area of design he will specialize, the budding designer-businessman must decide on the location and nature of his establishment. Depending on his chosen field, his capital, the geographic and economic characteristics of his community, and the image he wants to project, he may choose to set up his firm as a:

1. Home Studio,
2. Business Office, or
3. Retail Establishment.

1. **The Home Studio (or home office)**
   —a part of his residence set aside for his business—is the location most beginners think of first, and it should be reviewed in light of the following advantages and disadvantages:

   Advantages:
   a. Capital required is minimal, with practically no outlay for rent, decor, furnishings, equipment, and continuing overhead.

   b. If tastefully furnished, the designer's residence can serve as a showcase for his talents.

   c. It creates an aura favorable to a practice specializing in residential interiors.

   d. It solves certain special personal situations where the designer finds it difficult to absent himself or herself from home; obviously the prime case in point would be a woman with small children who either cannot afford or declines to leave them in the case of others.

   e. It may be the only possible location in small communities where suitable business premises do not exist.

   f. It may provide an ideal setting for the personal nature of designer-client relationships which are typical of certain small communities.

   g. From a tax viewpoint, a portion of the expenses of a home studio are proper deductions as business rent. These expenses should be assessed by the designer's accountant.

   Disadvantages:
   a. Since the image of a home studio does not sit well with businessmen, the home studio is not a helpful base to work from if the designer wants to do non-residential interiors. Businessmen prefer to work with "businessmen".

   b. The home studio looks suspiciously unbusinesslike to trade sources. Designers in major market areas are apt to find that trade sources will not welcome designers who appear to be involved in purchasing for themselves and their personal friends.

   c. The constant flow of clients, deliverymen, and employees can disrupt the private premises, and the areas subjected to traffic may be inadequate, resulting in unwieldy, irritating operations.

   d. In many communities zoning laws prohibit the use of a residence for business purposes.

2. **Business Office.**
   The successful operation of a business often depends upon the facade it presents to its clients. There is no question that a design office located in a good business area gives the impression of a sound and businesslike organization, particularly in metropolitan centers. This kind of set-up gives potential clients a feeling of security and prevents them from speculating that the

business is a part-time avocation.

The location of the office depends on conditions in the community. In cities where trade showrooms are centralized in a specific locality, it makes sense for the designer's office to be nearby, saving time and money in covering the market. If no trade showroom center exists, then obviously the factors to be considered in locating the office are convenience to clients or potential clients, and the attractiveness of the neighborhood.

Rental cost should be analyzed in relation to overall operating expenses and to the projected income with which the designer expects to pay his expenses. The lease should be reviewed by legal counsel to apprise the designer of his rights and possible liabilities.

It is also important for the designer to analyze the cash needed to alter the space if it will have to be altered, and to obtain essential furnishings and equipment. It is poor business judgment to bite off more than you can chew.

3. **Retail Establishment.**
In many suburban and rural communities, small home furnishings shops are the commonest settings for a design service, and for obvious reasons. The shop's open door is a natural attraction for potential clients. The retail sale of furnishings and accessories provide the designer with an income base and covers at least part of his overhead. Even in larger communities opening a shop is in certain ways the path of least resistance for a designer who wants to get started, because many people who are still unsophisticated about professional interior design service and timid about seeking it, will step into a shop without hesitation. If the designer-

entrepreneur can win the shopper's confidence, he may develop a future client.

It should not be necessary to add that running a shop is a business in itself. The traffic patterns and economic conditions of the location have crucial bearing on the designer's chances for success. And the "retail establishment" designer needs enough working capital to set up the shop and inventory a reasonable stock of furnishings and accessories. The amount of the designer's capital will be a determining factor in how much credit manufacturers and trade sources will extend to him.

Chapter Five

Securing Essential Counsel and Assistance

On plunging into practice, the neophyte will find himself confronted with problems beyond his ken, with decisions beyond his experience. As a rule this will occur not in the area of design but in the business aspects of his practice, since the business world can be a bewildering maze to the uninitiated. Even in the area of design the young member of the profession will, however, occasionally find himself in situations that call for competence not in his own but in some related field—in some profession such as architecture, landscape architecture, or engineering—or in some technical specialty such as lighting, heating and air-conditioning, plumbing, or so forth.

It is a cardinal rule in business that unknown territory should never be explored without a competent guide—a professional or specialist in *that* territory. It takes shrewdness to know one's own limitations, and insight to respect professionalism in fields distant from one's own.

The self-deluding amateur decorator who insinuates himself into the trade showrooms and who wastes time, energy, and money in the pathetic game of "getting it wholesale"—i.e. avoiding the expense of engaging a professional interior designer—is an excellent example for the inexperienced interior designer to bear in mind when he is tempted to cut corners by doing without professional advice. It is unrealistic. It invariably costs much more in the end. Retaining professional counsellors is the first step in launching a practice.

Also at the beginning the accountant should be consulted on the question of the most advantageous business formation for the company—individual form, partnership, or corporation—based on estimate of its effects on taxes and liabilities.

The Accountant

The way business is conducted throughout the civilized world today, it is practically impossible for any business—no matter how small—to operate without the services of a qualified accountant. In a small or medium-sized firm he is not likely to be a full-time employee but a consultant, though the firm may employ a bookkeeper or even a bookkeeping staff. The fact to understand is that the accountant is much more than a keeper of records or a sender of bills. In addition to his traditional functions pertaining to the maintenance and interpretation of properly kept records, the accountant is an indispensable management consultant and tax advisor—and is becoming more so each year.

At the outset the accountant should be consulted on the crucial question of the amount of capital which will be required for the contemplated business venture. Too many designers waste years of preparation in building a reputation and setting the stage for operations that are bound to die of attrition before they develop sufficiently to show a profit—simply because they have underestimated the operating capital required. Accountants experienced in the interiors field can give invaluable advice on how much money will be needed to secure necessary credit for stock and other costs, depending on the nature of the firm, the practice, and the community.

The accountant will organize the bookkeeping records and the office procedures and systems necessary for an intelligent control of the flow of operations.

He will register the new company with the necessary Federal, state, and local taxing authorities, so that compliance with the multitude of necessary taxes is assured. He will prepare or supervise the preparation of the various tax returns, and schedule for the timely filing of such returns.

It is necessary to point out that among the various taxes that businessmen are faced with, the sales tax is likely to pose many problems. If the designer's company is in a state or community where sales taxes are levied, it is of utmost importance that the accountant properly guide the interior designer as to what facets of his business dealings are subject to the billing and collection of sales taxes in his particular community. In taxable sales, the vender is responsible for the proper charging of the sales tax and for remitting the sums collected to the taxing authorities. Improper handling of this phase can lead to a heavy financial penalty though the vender is in effect a middleman charging and collecting from the ultimate consumer for the benefit of the taxing authority.

As the business gathers momentum, the accountant should be called upon for periodic financial statements and the analysis of such statements. This will give the interior designer an intelligent review of the financial results of his past operations—and guidance for the future. The accountant will relate the income and the operating overhead of the past and will be in a position to project overhead requirements for the future, to determine when and if changes in the fee structure might be desirable, and how fast the operation should expand or contract.

Legal Advisor

Legal counsel should be retained to effectuate the preliminary formalities of a new business in accordance with the law. After that the need for legal counsel will continue as legal decisions and formalities arise from time to time. If the new business is to be a partnership or corporation, an attorney must be retained to draw up the necessary legal documents. If the business is to be operated as an "individual form company", an attorney should be consulted about the legal limitations and form of operating under an assumed name, and the problems of unlimited liabilities. Legal guidance should be sought before signing a lease for business premises. An improper or misunderstood lease can wreak considerable damage on the finances or operations of a firm. There are related problems to be considered even if the firm is to be operated from the designer's residence and no leases are necessary, for zoning laws and restrictions must be checked to make sure that the designer's operations will not violate the law.

Banking Facilities

The new business venture should arrange for banking facilities close to the location of the office. The bank manager will be most helpful in setting up a commercial account. Such an account should be maintained only for the business and should not be commingled with personal deposits and disbursements. The initial capital deposit should be big enough to give the business an appearance of stability, for the bank may be called upon by trade sources for credit information on the designer.

Conversely, the bank can give the interior designer invaluable credit information about his own new clients.

It is virtually impossible for a business to operate without obtaining credit terms from trade sources; a new business would do well to register with the leading credit agencies. One of the following three should carry a listing on the company:

1. Allied Board of Trade, which functions as a clearing house of credit information about interior designers.

2. Lyon Furniture Mercantile Agency, which is best suited for interior designers who operate retail shops.
3. Dun and Bradstreet, a leading national credit agency.

As previously noted, the firm's accountant is the person best qualified to prepare credit registrations, since the financial status of the business is indicated, along with other pertinent facts.

Trade sources rely on credit agency reports and listings in determining the amount of credit they will advance to the interior designer.

Insurance Counsellor
A reputable insurance counsellor should be retained to survey the potential hazards to which the interior design firm might be subjected. It then becomes the counsellor's responsibility to provide an insurance program for protection against the eventualities. Obviously the scope of the program will vary with the size and complexity of the firm.

Proper insurance coverage is of utmost financial importance should an unforeseen casualty occur. Unnecessary and improper coverage can be expensive. In view of its importance, the subject is treated in greater detail in Chapter 24.

Technical Advisors and Collaborators in Related Fields
In developing certain interior design jobs, the designer may face problems which he is professionally or technically unqualified to solve because they are beyond the ordinary scope of interior design. Not all designers are alike in the range of their technical know-how, of course. There is considerable variation in the curricula of design schools, and no designer is given the same opportunities to

learn from experience as any other, so that the cut-off point of competence will vary in each instance. But there is hardly any designer who will not find himself there at one time or another. He will face a job calling for architectural plans of working drawings or electrical duct layouts, or ventilation system details, or specifications for heavy construction, or a general coordination of many different technical facilities that are definitely beyond him. He must establish working contacts with architects, electrical engineers, air-conditioning and ventilating experts, and good general contractors so that he will have collaborators ready when the need arises.

Part 2 Carrying Through a Job and Charging for it

Part 2 Carrying Through a Job and Charging for it

Chapter Six

Initial Contact with the Client

How the potential client comes upon the designer to whom he wants to offer a job—where and how designers and clients find each other—is beyond our scope. Here we are concerned not with whether the potential client was charmed by the designer's work or awed by his fame nor why he decided to seek out *that* particular designer—but *what happens next*. If the job hanging in the balance is to be successful for everyone involved, then this stage is crucial. A great deal depends on how the designer handles the first interview or interviews—that preliminary contact during which the client broaches the possibility of the job, shows the designer the premises, tells him what he wants and how much he is prepared to pay, and perhaps comes to terms with him about proceeding.

Regardless of whether it happens to a designer and client who are meeting for the first time or who are already acquainted with one another, the client's first expression of interest in having the designer do a job sets a familiar course of events into motion. Experience has shown that the designer should see to it that these events follow a fairly standardized pattern and include certain procedures—beginning with the first formal interview about the job.

A. **The first formal interview** should ideally be in the designer's studio, the setting which he has created for himself, among the effects and trappings which indicate his professionalism, facilities, talent, and artistic concerns. If the first interview turns out to be an inspection of the client's home by the designer, the designer must ask himself whether to charge for the time and cost of traveling on a first visit. It is the practice of many designers not to charge for the first interview if it takes place at the client's home, on the ground that this expense should be charged off as one of the costs of developing sales poten-

tial. Even if the cost is rationalized in this way, it is the writer's opinion that a visit to a place far from the designer's base should be charged for at a flat hourly or per diem rate sufficient to cover both the time and travel expense.

B. **The question of rapport** is important in all kinds of interior design, but it is absolutely crucial in residential work, where the very nature of the task requires that the designer spend a great deal of time in personal contact with the client. Versatility and flexibility are desirable qualities in interior designers, some of whom can do an amazing variety of work for many different kinds of clients. Nevertheless there are occasions when the obvious differences between clients and designers in such matters as taste, temperament, manners, and ideas about styles of living are so great that they are bound to disagree about interiors. In non-residential work it may be enough for the designer to stay within a specified mode or style and meet specified functional requirements in design, while being correct in carrying on the business transactions involved in the job, to insure that the job will proceed satisfactorily. But in residential work it is important that the very first meeting indicate strong rapport between client and designer. Without actually falling in love with each other, they should understand each other and be able to get along—and there has to be definite esthetic rapport as well. If the initial interview indicates mutual irritation, the designer should seriously consider the effects of taking on the client. It may be wiser not to go on.

C. **The designer's ability to sell himself** is essential if he wants a firm of his own. From the first the designer must not only inspire confidence, but give the client tangible clues that he is likely to meet the client's conception of what he wants. Even if the client has seen a little of the designer's work, he may not grasp that the designer can do many things. It is important to have pictures of completed work to show. Sketches are better than nothing, black-and-white photographs are more convincing than sketches but fail in the important requirement of showing color. Models are very impressive indeed, but designers in the residential field have relatively little occasion to prepare them. Color photographs, and above all color slides, are ideal. A library of stereoscopic color slides can beautifully record many interiors and can be stored in a small space. Projection can give an effective idea of the three-dimensional reality, size, and color.

There is no substitute, of course, for showing actual installations, but it takes valuable time and is not always easy to arrange if the occupants resent intrusions of their privacy or are not maintaining their premises tidily. But where a big job is hanging in the balance, a guided tour may be essential to enable the client to make up his mind.

D. **The danger of overselling** at the first meeting is real if the designer is eager to get the job and quick to develop ideas. The classic example of what can happen occurs when the potential client brings a set of floor plans and other concrete material and information as a basis for discussion. It has often happened that enthusiastic designers have rushed into long and detailed descriptions of their proposed solutions immediately, going so far as to sketch furniture layouts, put together color schemes and fabric and paint samples, and show photographs of furniture, drapery treatments, carpeting, and other elements. If the potential client is on a

brain-picking expedition, the designer has served him well. Many "clients" have been known to interview designer after designer, collecting a vast fund of ideas and suggestions. And many have been known to transform themselves into instant decorators, doing their own buying and installing, following the suggestions stolen from their unwary victims. The experienced designer goes just so far and no further in making specific suggestions to a client who has not yet retained him and is still just shopping around.

E. **Defining the scope of services** is one of the important things to be accomplished at the first interview. The designer must find out what services the client wants, the full breadth of the job, and the client's budgeting base. If the budget is unrealistic for the results expected by the client, the designer should inform him of this at once, and if the client cannot or will not adjust his thinking, the designer should step away before he starts. Another instance where the designer should back out of the picture occurs when the client outlines esthetic concepts which are beyond the designer's capabilities or the natural direction of his talent. The designer should never lose sight of the fact that if he takes on jobs he knows are not for him, he is risking his reputation as well as his pocketbook.

F. **Defining the firm's financial methods** is another thing that needs to be taken care of at the initial interview. The potential client should be advised of the firm's business procedures and its methods of charging. The points to be covered include the letter of agreement, the retainer, the deposits required for purchase orders, the method and timing of billing, and the fee basis. It is as important for the client

New Project Check List—Residential

Company Name

Date _____

Designer _____

Client		Husband	Wife
	(Last Name)	(Initial)	(First Name)	(First Name)

Street _____ Install Address _____

City & State _____ City & State _____

Telephone _____ Telephone _____

Business Affiliation _____ Referred by _____

Design Information _____

Areas Involved — Scope of Services _____

_____

_____

_____

Type of Design Desired (Style, Color, etc.) _____

_____

_____

Husband's Business or Profession _____

Children (No., Age, Sex) _____

Allergies or Handicaps _____ Pets _____

Social Activities (Describe) _____

_____

Estimated Budget _____

Credit Check _____

Deposit or Retainer _____

Fee Basis _____

_____

Expenses Reimbursed _____

Installation Date Requested _____

Travel Directions _____

_____

Other Comments _____

_____

Form No. 1   (To obtain forms, see page 10.)

to have as much information as possible about the designer and his business methods as it is for the designer to know as much as possible about the potential client.

G. **The "New Project Check List"** shown on page 37 is helpful in collecting and clarifying some of the essential information about the client referred to in the preceding lines. Interior design is not a simple sales transaction, but a series of personal interactions and communications between two parties who are producing a complex work of art—an intimate personal environment for an individual or group of individuals. Here is one suggestion for the form on which information can be entered during the initial interview.

Chapter Seven

Letter of Agreement

When—as a result of the first or second interview—the client expresses his wish to retain the designer and the designer accepts the assignment, immediate recognition must be given to the business and financial responsibilities assumed by both parties. Serious friction over the designer's artistic performance in a job is relatively rare; the client's choice of the designer is in itself stimulated by his admiration for other examples of the designer's work, and the initial interviews and presentations give the client ample opportunity to size up the designer's proposals before making his decision. The area where friction and misunderstanding frequently crop up is in the financial and operational transactions involved.

To avoid unresolved misunderstandings, with all their attendant unpleasantness, financial risks, and possibilities for scandal and legal action, the relationship between client and designer on each and every job must be spelled out in a letter of agreement. This letter specifies the exact services that are to be rendered by the designer as well as the conditions under which the services are to be rendered, and it formalizes the client's acceptance of these services and the amount and timing of his payment for them.

Today the scope of interior design service is so broad and varied, and the conditions particular to each job also so varied, that it is virtually impossible to formalize all conditions in a standard letter of agreement. It is therefore necessary for the designer to be aware of the logical components of letters of agreement, so he can prepare one for each job that comes up in his practice, and cover every contingency important in that job.

The universal commercial code which has been adopted in most states with variations provides that contracts for the sale of goods for the price of $500. or more are not enforceable unless there is some writing sufficient to indicate that a contract of sale has been made between the parties and signed by the party against whom enforcement is sought. There are exceptions including an exception for goods specially manufactured for the buyer not suitable for sale to others. Certain other types of agreements may be void unless in writing and signed by the party to be charged under the statute of frauds, such as an agreement which by its terms is not to be performed within one year from the making thereof.

A writing is effective as an agreement if it contains a statement of the essential terms of the bargain with reasonable accuracy and is signed by the party to be charged. The writing may be in the form of a letter and still be a binding contract if it meets these requirements. But a writing which leaves out a description of the goods to be sold or fails to identify the parties may not be a sufficient memorandum.

The most important points that should be covered in every letter of agreement are the following:

1. **Scope of Services**
   A complete description of the services which the designer is to render and identification of the area of premises to which such services will pertain. It is necessary to be specific in this description to avoid future disagreement as to what the client "thought" the designer was going to do and to be responsible for.

2. **Deposit or Retainer**
   It should be customary for the designer to obtain a deposit or a retainer fee before starting a job. The purposes and uses of such deposits and retainers are as follows:

39

A. *Retainer as a Deposit*

The retainer as a deposit is not an additional fee to the designer but is requested from the client at the inception of the job and credited to the client's account at the end of the job, or during specified phases of the job. This retainer deposit is a must, since it will protect the designer's expenditure of time and effort in the initial stages of work should the client decide to drop his services. It is customary in a letter of agreement (or contract) between the designer and the client for the designer to request a "retainer deposit" which is to be applied to the designer's time charges should the client terminate the agreement before completion. A retainer deposit also serves as a "go ahead" signal to a designer to begin the first phase of a job. It is poor business to waste time, effort, and money in the hope that a job contract will materialize. The designer should not begin until a retainer deposit has been received.

B. *Retainer as a Fee*

Many designers consider it sound business practice to be paid a fee for the initial study and planning of a project, separate and distinct from any other fee involved in the job. This fee is collected before work begins, and is treated as payment for the designer's (preliminary) services. The size of the fee must be based upon the nature of the job, the amount of time and effort involved in the initial phase, and the budget for the job.

C. *Deposits on Estimates or Contracts*

Some designers develop a complete estimate, both for the design concept and the budget on the job, at the inception, and ask a deposit (such as one-third of the total budget) before beginning the actual ordering of services and goods for a client. The balance is to be paid to the designer in additional installments (for example, one-third after orders are placed, and the balance upon installation of the job).

3. **Manner of Payment**

The letter of agreement should clearly state the manner and time sequence of payments to be made to the designer for goods or services delivered to the client. If the designer's compensation is a fixed fee, a schedule of payments should be stated indicating:

a. ....% on signing the letter of agreement

b. ....% on acceptance of design concept

c. ....% on completion of installation

It should be a matter of policy to have the final installment as small an amount as possible.

If the designer is not working on a fixed fee but on a mark-up of merchandise provided to the client, then the agreement should indicate the amount of deposit required before placing orders, with the balance to be paid upon delivery of the item or, the installation of the various items of furnishings and services.

4. **Confirmations of Purchase Proposals**

The letter of agreement should state that the designer will place orders for goods and services only upon receipt of confirmations for such orders signed by the client and accompanied by the client's check for the required deposit. (The underlying theory of confirmations, their provisions, manner of preparation and use, together with examples of typical forms are covered in Chapter 8.)

5. **Fee or Compensation Base**

A complete description of the basis for the setting of the fees which the designer is charging the client for his services—whether the fee is a fixed sum, a percentage of costs, or the retail price of goods and services—should be set forth and clearly understood by the client. (The various methods of setting fees and compensations for the designer are covered in Chapter 9.)

6. **Services and Goods from Others than the Designer's own Designated Sources**

Usually the designer's purchases for the client will be made by him through his own sources, and services for their client will also be executed by his own staff or by work rooms, craftsmen, and contractors who perform the work to the designer's order, thereby giving the designer control of prices, mark-ups, and the resulting compensation to him—not to mention giving him control of the quality of the merchandise or workmanship. However, if the designer is to submit plans and purchase specifications and the client is to use trade sources selected by the client over whom the designer has no control, provision must be made:

1. Waiving the designer's responsibility for the satisfactory execution of such orders, and
2. Specifying the designer's compensation for his service in designing, planning, and specifying everything covered by such orders.

It is essential that the letter of agreement contain a statement "that where the client uses his own sources, the designer is to be paid his fee—either on the basis of a percentage of the cost of the item or service or as a set fee for all such purchases made as a result of the designer's plans, specifications, or choice of furnishings." Further, this statement should include a disclaimer of responsibility for work done by other than the designer's own workrooms or trade sources.

Services by others are not a problem if the designer is working for a fixed fee to cover the entire job, since, when he establishes the amount of this fee, he will take into consideration all of the services he will perform. The problem assumes importance only when the designer is working on a retail mark-up compensation basis.

7. **Extra Services**

The letter of agreement covers the scope of services. Occasionally the client may request additional services *after* signing the letter of agreement; or he may change his mind about some facet of the job *afterwards,* or change his mind about some item or service to be purchased *after* he has given his signed confirmation in approval of one or more of such purchases. Such changes are among the costliest burdens which can arise in a designer's practice, involving the designer's time and that of his staff in re-designing, re-specifying, re-ordering, or for cancelling orders and compensating trade sources. Or the designer may find that he or his staff have invested time in an area of the job that will not be carried out and that the client therefore does not intend to pay for. Or the designer may find himself in the position of being asked to do more services for a fixed fee than he had taken into consideration when he had set that fee.

To protect him against the financial burdens that may thus be inflicted by a client's afterthoughts, the letter of agreement should state that "the designer will be entitled to additional compensation for services requested that are not covered by the agreement, and for

41

costs and expenses incurred by the designer as a result of changes made by the client after he has given his approval."

The method of compensation for extras can be based upon a percentage mark-up on the cost of purchases or services involved, or it can be a fee to cover the total estimated time required to design and prepare specifications for the changes and additions, or it can be an hourly rate to cover the extra work.

8. **Freight Charges**
If the freight, shipping, or cartage costs are not included in the price quoted to the client, the letter of agreement should clearly state that all such charges will be billed to the client as a separate and distinct charge and that the client will be responsible for reimbursement of such charges to the designer.

Many clients do not understand or appreciate the extent of cartage and freight charges that must be paid in the moving of furniture and other items either from source to the client's premises or from premises to workshops and back again. Because items may have to be processed several items—drapery fabrics going from fabric house to a processor who applies protective and fireproofing finishes or treatments and then to the workroom—and furniture going to the upholsterer—and because many furnishings are either heavy or fragile or both, freight and cartage are costly items and can create problems. Therefore, it is best to make a definite point of advising the client about them at the inception of a job, and covering them in the letter of agreement.

9. **Sales Taxes**
If the designer or the client is in a sales tax area, the letter should state that sales taxes, where applicable, will be charged the client and remitted to the designer, who has the responsibility for collecting them and remitting them to the taxing authority.

10. **Reimbursement of Expenses**
The designer's preliminary analysis of the job's scope of services and location will indicate whether he will incur extraordinary travel expenses, blueprint charges, long-distance telephone charges, or special expenses occasioned by the site or location. If conditions which may entail special expenses of any kind can arise, it is best for the letter of agreement to spell out the designer's position as to reimbursement for them.

11. **Other Conditions**
Among other conditions which may arise in a job and which should be covered in the letter of agreement are:

a. Conditions covering consultation with architects,

b. Conditions covering the execution of presentations,

c. Conditions covering cancellation of certain phases of the work,

d. Conditions covering disputes which may arise,

e. Conditions covering guarantees of durability of merchandise selected by the designer,

f. Conditions covering the cancellation of orders by the client after the designer has placed such orders,

g. Conditions covering the ownership of the designer's plans, layouts, and specifications.

In summary: The designer should carefully study all the circumstances of the job as well as his prospective client's character before writing the letter of agreement, because in actual practice the letter is the designer's proposal and his tool for securing maximum harmony and minimum confusion in the performance of a job. Once signed by the client, it becomes an effective protection on every point covered in the provisions; every point which the conditions of the job or the client's character may require had better be there.

On page 44 is a typical letter of agreement prepared for a residential interior design job in which estimates and purchases are specified as the various phases of the job proceed in orderly steps:

As stated previously, some designers prepare a complete estimate at the inception of a job and request the client's signed confirmation with a deposit of one-third of the total estimated cost. If the job is to be done on this basis, the letter of agreement should say so, substituting such paragraphs for the second and last paragraphs in the sample letter of agreement—the paragraphs covering confirmations and the original retainer deposit.

The legal status of the letter of agreement—that is, how binding it is in case of dispute—is covered in paragraphs four and five of this chapter .

What about a printed contract? Even if the letter of agreement is sufficiently binding, would it nevertheless be advisable to have a printed contract or standard form?

The standard form or printed contract *has* made its way into use and acceptance in the interior de-

sign field. There are some who contend that standardizing contractual relationships is effective in lessening or in altogether removing the possibility of errors of omission or commission. If the designer wants to use Standard Form Contracts in his practice, he should have his attorney work one out very carefully after duly considering the many facets of the designer's practice and methods of operating.

The Standard Form Contract has to be broad enough to cover all of the essential points described in this chapter. The desirability of using Standard Form Contracts in interior design practice has been argued because of their one basic weakness: No two designing jobs are likely to be similar in scope of service, method of installation, fee arrangement, or a host of other facets. A short, concise Standard Form Contract cannot cover the many points relevant to any particular job. A long legal document that attempts to cover every conceivable contingency is likely to be so weighed down with technical and legal verbiage as to frighten the layman into refusing to sign—at least until he has in turn had legal counsel review the contract. The expense of retaining an attorney and the time involved in legal negotiations, although undoubtedly invaluable per se to both client and designer, may often discourage the client from proceeding in any case.

The letter of agreement, on the other hand, can be made to conform to the requirements of each job, and while it has the necessary legal force, its form and language are those of everyday business correspondence familiar to most clients. It is helpful to both parties because it spells out not only the responsibilities of the client, but the responsibilities of the designer—a point which should be emphasized in discussions with clients.

If the client refuses to sign the letter of agreement, the designer is better off without the job.

<u>TYPICAL LETTER OF AGREEMENT</u>

DATE _____

Mr. & Mrs. John Smith
1 First Street
New York, New York

Dear Mr. & Mrs. Smith:

As is my custom I wish to advise you that a retainer of $ *500* is
required to authorize my proceeding with the execution of plans, layout and
Design Concepts to be submitted for your approval and the furnishing of your living
room, dining room, foyer and master bedroom of your new apartment at 2 Second Street,
Apt. 1-B.

All purchases made through this office will be billed to you at retail
prices. Purchases to be made will be submitted to you for your approval in the
form of confirmations annexed hereto which confirmation will require your signature
and a fifty percent deposit to authorize the placement of such orders. The month
of payment of the balance of the purchase price will be set forth in each confirmation.

Alterations, detailed construction or purchases made directly by you
as a result of plans submitted by my office but executed by tradespeople other than
my own indicated sources or workrooms must be approved by my office or (responsibility
of workmanship executed by tradespeople other than my selected workrooms will be
assumed by you) and become subject to a *10* % commission fee to be paid to me by you
to cover my designing time and supervision.

All cartage, freight charges and sales taxes will be payable by you.

You shall reimburse me for travel expenses, blueprints, telephone toll
charges or other extraordinary expenses incurred as a result of your instructions as
well as any costs incurred by my office as a result of changes made by you after
plans and specifications have been approved.

In the event this assignment is terminated before completion the retainer
will be applied as compensation for services rendered to the extent of the cost
of such services based upon our regular hourly charges. (see footnote)

3

If you consent to the Letter of Agreement please sign and return one copy of this letter to this office together with the retainer.

Very truly yours,

_____
Signature

ACCEPTED _____

_____
Signature

_____
Signature

Footnote: omit

This paragraph may be broadened out for clarification purposes depending upon the situation.

In the event this assignment is terminated before completion (completion to be described) as:

1. Purchase of minimum of $_____ of furnishings and services.

2. Completion and acceptance of the design concept, if the job is purely in that category and no purchases are contemplated.

3. Any other description which will indicate what is to be considered "completion of the job".

Then, the retainer will be applied to compensate me for my time expended at the rate of $_____ per hour. Any balance of the retainer will be returned to you and should the retainer be insufficient to cover the cost of my time such additional amount will be billed to you.

Chapter Eight

Confirmation of Purchase Proposals

In the preceding chapter we referred to "confirmation of purchases by a designer on behalf of his client." The confirmation has come into use particularly in the residential field because most designers, under the conditions of designing residential interiors, find it impossible to write an estimate at the inception of the job that will cover *every* item and service, together with its actual cost.

The use of confirmations makes it possible to keep the original letter of agreement or contract relatively simple and concise in language and content, for the confirmations serve in effect as subsidiary contracts which spell out all details that present themselves in the job after the original letter of agreement has been written and signed.

Let us examine what a confirmation accomplishes: When a designer selects merchandise or completes the plans or design specifications for custom-made items, it is essential that he secure the client's written agreement before proceeding with the purchase or with the order for the work. This is done by delivering to the client some form of written instrument which completely describes the proposed purchase or custom item in full detail including the cost to the client. It makes sense then to require that the client, if he accepts the proposal, should return to the designer a signed copy of the paper, signifying his confirmation of the proposal.

If the item has been properly described in the proposal, the client has the right to expect it and to hold the designer responsible for its delivery. If the item delivered is as described in the proposal, the client has no right to refuse to accept it or to refuse to accept liability for the purchase made in his behalf. By preparing confirmations for every purchase and order needed for the job, the designer is protected because the client has been fully advised as to the nature and cost of each item, and has given his signed approval of it.

But there is one additional requirement which must be made before the confirmation on each item is considered complete, and it is crucial: a *deposit* from the client must be returned with the signed confirmation.

It has been pointed out that some designers make it a practice to require a sizable deposit with the signing of the contract. For example, if the proposed budget for the entire job is $10,000., the designer will expect a deposit somewhere in the vicinity of $3,000. This is unquestionably an excellent way to begin a job. However, it has been found that many clients are loath to give this much at the beginning of the job, and would much prefer giving deposits as purchasing proceeds. Therefore, since it is an absolute necessity for the designer to adhere to the "deposit principle", there is no better way to proceed than to request that the client pay the deposit for each specific purchase when he returns the signed confirmation.

The majority of successful interior designers adhere strictly to the "deposit principle" in residential practice because:

1. When a client sends a fifty percent payment for an item or service, you, the designer, can be well assured that he has made up his mind that this is what he wants, so that the rejection of delivered goods will be held at a minimum.

2. Obtaining of the client's deposit funds will keep the balance of his accounts receivable at a decent level.

3. Few designers have sufficient capital to meet the deposit or payment requirements set in the credit terms of trade sources. Clients' deposits

serve as working capital during the period between ordering for the client and finally collecting from the client.

4. The "deposit principle" safeguards against excessive losses caused by irresponsible clients. The following example illustrates this point: Assume that the designer works on the retail basis and that he is purchasing a sofa for the client.

List Price	$600.
Cost to designer (40% off)	360.
Deposit requested from client (50% of list price)	300.

Should the client default in accepting delivery, the worst that can happen to the designer is that he will lose $60., the difference between his cost of $360. and the deposit of $300. he has received.

A confirmation can be prepared for the purchase of a single item or more than one. Depending upon the size of the job and the purchasing habits of the designer, it is not unusual to find a sizable volume of paper work involved in processing the great number of confirmations involved in a single job, but the benefits of the confirmation system more than make up for the expense and work entailed.

The confirmation should be prepared in triplicate. Two copies are to be sent to the client with instructions to return one signed copy together with the required deposit to the designer's office, and one copy to be retained by the client for his records. One copy is to be retained in the designer's office as a record of outstanding confirmations and then matched to the signed copy returned by the client.

After the signed copy has been returned by the client, the confirmation can then be used as a guide for the preparation of purchase orders.

In the confirmation system it is essential to emphasize that Purchase Orders are *not* sent to vendors *until the confirmation and deposit are returned to the designer's office*. Following this rule will avoid conflicts with trade sources over the cancellation of premature orders. The expenses caused by charges for the cancellation of orders are difficult to pass on to a client unless the cancellation can be pinpointed directly to the client's own action. If a confirmation of order has been signed and cancellation then follows, obviously the fault lies with the client. If there is no confirmation of purchase, the client can easily deny that he gave the designer a verbal instruction to purchase, and thus relieve himself of resulting liabilities.

The sample forms reproduced in the rest of this chapter are good models from which to develop a confirmation form suited to the particular needs of a design office.

Following the forms, which are on pages 48–51, the reader will find a brief evaluation of each one (page 52). Throughout the book, incidentally, lettering on the back of any form is printed as an extra page here. Thus the back of Form No. 2 appears on page 49, following the front reproduced on page 48.

A

Proposal Contract

Company Name
Address

To:

We are pleased to submit this agreement for proposed work as follows:

Terms:

50 per-cent deposit of proposal due on acceptance. Balance due on completion of any orders.

Name of Company

By: _____

If you wish us to proceed with this work, kindly sign and return copy, retaining original for your record.

Accepted: Date:

_____   _____
                                                 (See Terms and Conditions of Agreement on reverse side)

Form No. 2   (To obtain forms, see page 10.)

Terms and Conditions

1. Orders for articles, materials or contractor's services will not be placed in work until signed confirmation of PROPOSAL CONTRACT is received, together with any required deposit.

2. Prices of materials, articles and contractor's services are subject to change. Before proceeding with order notice of any price increase will be given and confirmation of revised price required.

3. Prices do not include shipping, freight and trucking charges or insurance in transit, all of which will be at Client's expense.

4. Orders approved under this contract are non-cancellable.

A

5. All orders for materials, articles and contractor's services shall be placed by Designer solely on Client's credit.

6. Prices do not include sales or other applicable taxes.

7. No responsibility is assumed for delays occasioned by failure of others to meet commitments or for any other reason or cause beyond Designer's control.

8. Designs, samples, drawings and specifications shall remain Designer's property, whether or not the work for which they are made be executed.

9. Designer does not guarantee any fabric, material or article against wearing, fading or latent defect, but to extent permitted by law, Client shall have benefit at Client's sole expense in the assertion thereof, of all guarantees and warranties possessed by Designer against suppliers and manufacturers.

10. Furnishing or installing of any or all materials or articles is subject to Designer's ability to obtain the same and to procure the necessary labor therefor and is contingent on strikes, accidents or other causes beyond Designer's control.

11. If Designer is required to render services not contemplated by this agreement or incurs extra drafting or other expenses due to changes ordered by Client or other cause, Designer shall be paid for such extra services and expenses the reasonable value or cost thereof.

Form No. 2

B

Confirmation

Company Name
Address

To _____   Date _____

Address _____

_____

Quantity	Details	Unit	Price	Total
	Dear			
	So that we may proceed with this order as soon as possible, will you please sign the original copy of this confirmation and return to us, together with your check made payable to .... for the amount of .... for the 50% deposit required.			
	Thank you for your valued order and your attention to this matter.			

Terms:
1. AMOUNT OF DEPOSIT_____ BALANCE DUE UPON COMPLETION OF
   THIS ORDER. ORDERS ARE NOT PUT TO WORK UNTIL THIS ACKNOWLEDGMENT
   IS SIGNED AND RETURNED WITH DEPOSIT.
2. All bills payable 5 days after date of delivery.   ACCEPTED:
3. All delivery charges are additional.
4. Subject to Sales Tax and Federal Excise Tax when applicable. _____
                                                                Signature

Form No. 3   (To obtain forms, see page 10.)

Confirmation

Company Name
Address

To _____   Date _____

Address _____

_____

C

Quantity	Details	Unit	Price	Total
	Dear			
	We have already proceeded with this order, but in keeping with the customary requirements, will you please sign the original copy of this confirmation and return to us, together with your check for the one-third deposit in the amount of			
	Thank you for your valued order and your attention to this matter.			

Terms:
1. AMOUNT OF DEPOSIT_____ BALANCE DUE UPON COMPLETION OF THIS ORDER. ORDERS ARE NOT PUT TO WORK UNTIL THIS ACKNOWLEDGMENT IS SIGNED AND RETURNED WITH DEPOSIT.
2. All bills payable 5 days after date of delivery.   ACCEPTED:
3. All delivery charges are additional.
4. Subject to Sales Tax and Federal Excise Tax when applicable. _____
                                                                 Signature

Form No. 4 (To obtain forms, see page 10.)

Exhibit A

is a good form since it includes as part of the confirmation certain stipulations discussed in Chapter 7 on the Letter of Agreement (as the client's responsibility to pay for freight costs, sales taxes, cancellation, extra services, etc.).

Exhibit B

While this form does not include all the terms and conditions set forth in Exhibit A, its physical presentation and layout are excellent.

Exhibit C

is used by the design firm to cover any purchase which for some reason must be ordered immediately after having been verbally approved by the client.

Chapter Nine

Methods of Determining Fees and Compensations

How should an interior designer charge for his services? On what basis should he arrive at the amount of money due him for each interior he designs and executes?

This is the most controversial, most hotly debated, most coyly handled, most misunderstood, and most important problem facing the profession as a whole and the interior designer as an individual—if he wants a reasonable income in exchange for the talent, training, and time he invests in his life's work.

Often placed on the defensive, a great proportion of the qualified interior designers in the profession have spent far too much energy trying to prove that they do not make it a habit to rob the client blind. They would be well advised to use that energy, instead, for developing a rational method of handling the money side of their operations.

The issue of professionalism has in itself beclouded the problem of establishing proper fees and compensations. The argument goes that interior designers should stop acting like merchants who sell goods and begin to emulate physicians who charge a flat fee for their skill or musicians who charge for each performance or are engaged by the season. It cannot be denied that the basic commodity sold by the interior designer is compounded of such intangibles as skill and imagination, but no observer can close his eyes to the reality that the most "purely" professional fee systems—those based on the flat and hourly fee—have never dominated the field and are not gaining ground in proportion to the rapid growth in the volume of activity. There are good and sufficient reasons why this is so, although the flat and time fee systems work well enough for a small percentage of designers in the field for a small part of their practice. It is fundamentally irrelevant to equate the method of charging for the

design and execution of an interior with the method of charging for an operatic performance simply because both are professional activities.

The triumphant tenor who brings down the roof of the Met week after week gets the highest fee per performance. Artistic success equals financial success. Simple.

But many an interior designer who witnesses one esthetic triumph after another finds himself deeper in the red after every job. Artistic success equals financial failure? Obviously not so simple.

What *does* determine whether the designer will or will not make the grade financially?

More than any other factor, his ability to earn a proper financial return—assuming his competence as an interior designer—revolves principally upon his ability to establish a proper base or method for arriving at fees or compensations.

The bases or methods for computing fees and compensations which are in use today have been developed over decades by trial and error. These bases or methods can and do bring adequate financial returns to the designers who know when to use each one and who handle the procedures involved with sound business techniques.

But though this chapter describes the many methods or bases for computing fees, it is up to the reader to find the right one for each of his jobs. No one method is right for every firm or for every job done by any firm. There can be no standard method because there is no such thing as a standard job. Interior design is a highly unstandardized personal service. Different types of firms render different types of services to different types of clients in different types of communities in different geographical areas of the country—and *every* variable enters into the fee picture.

To rationally arrive at a fee or compensation base the interior designer must have a thorough grasp of:

1. His own operation, overhead, and income requirements.
2. The scope of services for each job.
3. The types of fee and compensation bases in use in the field, and how to apply the correct base depending upon his analysis of each job.

1. His Own Operation, Overhead, and Income Requirements:

Proper bookkeeping records must be maintained to afford an analysis of the costs of operation. Professionally interpreted financial statements can relate the costs of operation to the income dollar earned and to the labor dollar expended, thus giving a dollar-and-cents picture of the effectiveness of the base being used in covering operational overhead and profit. This is not quite as simple as it sounds, because in the interiors field there is generally no steady flow of repetitive business from which to deduce an estimate of operating costs. The interior design firm cannot be compared to a store where customers arrive in a predictable number to purchase specified merchandise upon which specific mark-ups over the cost have been placed in order to set the retail prices. Nor can the interior design firm be compared to the firm of an accountant or lawyer whose clients are retained on an annual basis. Interior design is non-repetitive. The designer completes an installation for a client without knowing whether he will ever see a similar job again. For this reason even the interior design firm which is too small to have a comptroller or financial advisor should retain the services of someone who will be in a position to interpret the results of the operation.

Along with the general books are two auxiliary types of records which should be maintained in order to accumulate the statistical information most helpful for guidance in setting up proper fees and compensations:

a. *Job cost records*
Every job should be analyzed to indicate its financial results after its completion: the gross income, costs, time expended, the cost of such expended time, and the net profit. This type of information will measure the financial success of each job, since the designer will be able to relate the amount of time expended to the profits earned, thereby discovering whether he earned a dollar an hour or twenty dollars an hour for his efforts. It will show him what types of jobs are profitable and what types of jobs he should avoid. It will also indicate what budget base he can assume in a job and still end up with a profit. (Very small budgets can result in very small profits, and the designer who takes on too many small-budget jobs may find himself wasting his time.)

b. *Time records*
Since all that the designer actually sells is talent and time, time is a crucial factor. The maintenance of accurate time records enables the designer to:

1. Relate time requirements to new jobs he is undertaking,

2. Relate time to the progress of his current jobs (and, therefore, to the amount of money

for time expended which the job is costing him),

3. Relate time to the completed job and the resulting profit.

The theory, objectives, and methods of recording time are discussed in greater depth in Chapter 23.

2. **The scope of services for each particular job:**

This is unquestionably the basic factor in arriving at a proper fee or compensation base.

How can the designer quote a fee without analyzing the job first? How can the designer say, "I work on a retail basis" or on a "cost-plus" basis or "for a fee of $_____ an hour" without first knowing the scope of services he is to perform and the profit he estimates he will make? Yet, this is what many designers do.

Shouldn't the designer first analyze the scope of the job? Shouldn't he first ask: What does this job entail?

a. Basically to create a *design concept* with very little in purchasing?

b. To produce a *design concept* and *complete the installation, purchasing* all required furnishings, materials, and services?

c. Will he have to spend time with contractors or architects?

d. Will he be purchasing from regular trade sources or will he have to prepare special construction specifications necessitating drafting-board time?

e. Is there a costly travel expense factor in the job?

f. Are there any unusual job-site problems?

g. If the job is a long distance from home, what problems and expenses may be presented by local trade sources, tariffs, and freight and delivery charges?

The client's budget for the job has been mentioned as one of the factors to be abstracted through a study of the designer's books. It also has an important bearing as a factor in this section, *the scope of services for each job.* Jobs for which the client has a small budget tend to be less profitable than those with a bigger budget. If the budget is smaller than a certain sum, the designer is well-advised to turn down the job. The question is: smaller than what sum?—and the answer is different for every firm. It pays to be diligent in getting an accurate answer and it is necessary to be strict in following the guideline thus indicated. The effect of the client's budget is analyzed in greater depth in Chapter 11.

3. **What Fees and Compensation Systems are Available? How Should One Determine Which to Use?**

1. Retail Basis
2. Cost Plus Percentage Mark-up
3. Percentage Off Retail
4. Flat Fee
5. Flat Fee Plus Percentage of Cost
6. Hourly or Per-Diem Fee

1. *Retail Basis*
The retail basis is best described as the billing for merchandise provided to a client at the list

price suggested by sources, where such list prices are available. Where list prices are not available, the manufacturer's net price to the designer is marked up to bring the article into the local competitive price range. This mark-up percentage can generally be assumed to be in the area of 70% to 100% on the manufacturer's net price. *This is unquestionably the most remunerative method of compensation to a designer,* since the difference between the cost of goods to the designer at net is substantially lower than the billing price at retail to the client. This method is used by the major interior design firms specializing in residential work in typical residential interiors where the cost of time involved in the design and installation factors is not too great, and the preponderance of the client's budget is set aside for the purchase of goods and services.

One actual and typical residential installation at retail shows the following figures:

Billing to Client	$27,827.
Merchandise at Cost	$15,298.
Construction Costs	2,791.
Actual Cost (exclusive of design time)	18,089.
Gross Profit	9,738.
% of Gross Profit to Billing Price	35%

These figures can be compared to the analysis of another residential job in which labor and construction involved amounted to a greater proportion of the budget than the furnishing of materials. (It is to be noted that there is no *retail price* for construction but simply a mark-up on the cost of construction.) :

Billing to Client	$124,105.
Merchandise at Cost	$35,973.
Construction Costs	58,420.
Miscellaneous Costs	1,384.
Actual Cost (exclusive of design time)	95,787.
Gross Profit	28,318.
% of Gross Profit to Billing Price	22.8%

Thus we can immediately see that the profit return is affected by the amount of merchandise purchased for the client. Preliminary analysis of the job estimates must be made to indicate the profit return. This profit return is then further analyzed as to the estimated amount of design time to be expended for the job.

The designer attempting to work on a retail basis will find that the method is *not* reasonable in a job that consists mostly of custom construction, design unrelated to the selection of merchandise, the preparation of floor plans or layouts, color specifications, the preparation of working drawings or specifications for construction or architectural details or alterations, with the budget devoted mainly to those items rather than to the purchase of furnishings. Thus, for the second example tabulated above, a design fee should have been added to bring the Gross Profit up to a reasonable figure of 35%.

If design unrelated to purchases constitutes the major function of the job, then the designer must determine an additional or alternative method of arriving at a proper compensation for the proposed work. In this event it would be correct to set a flat fee or hourly charge to compensate for the time allocated to the design phase, adding that to the retail billing for the furnishings purchased on behalf of the client.

2. *Cost Plus Percentage Mark-Up*

In this method, the designer's compensation for services rendered is arrived at by adding an agreed percentage to the actual cost of materials purchased for the client. The mark-up percentages utilized in the residential field ranges between 20% and 30%. It is a simple method of working with a client, but in its simplicity, it is also the *least remunerative*.

The failure to realize sufficient gross profit under this method can readily be illustrated by the following example:

Manufacturer's List Price (sofa)	$900.
Cost to Interior Designer (40% off)	540.
Designer's Mark-up (25% on cost)	135.

This method does not provide a profit margin capable of generating the funds required to maintain staff, pay overhead expenses, and properly compensate the designer for his time, talent, and effectiveness in producing a better than ordinary installation.

It would be remiss not to point out that this method of compensation is much used in many parts of the country. A segment of the design community is leery of basing its charges on the retail price for fear of competition from hungrier designers and department stores. It is typically used by young designers trying to attract a following. And the fact must be faced that the *cost plus percentage mark-up* basis literally gives away the designer's talent and effort in return for a financial return which

cannot support his business.

If this method *must* be used, it should be used in combination with other fee factors to insure reasonable compensation for services rendered. Variations which might be considered are:

a. *Cost plus a percentage mark-up* in addition to *an hourly charge* (e.g. $20-$30 per hour) for the time spent in developing the design concept, layouts, and consultations.

b. *Using the client's budget to* determine the extent to which the cost-plus system will be used. It can, for example, be decided that:

Budgets under $10,000. will be charged at *Retail*

Budgets over $10,000. will be charged at *Retail* on first $10,000. and a percent on cost for the rest.

3. *Percentage Off Retail*

In recent years another method for determining a fee has evolved. It is based on the manufacturer's suggested list price less 10%. The following example describes the method and the resulting profit:

List Price	$900.
Less 10%	90.
Billing Price to Client	810.
Cost to Designer	540.
Gross Profit to Designer	270.

Comparing this method to the cost plus 25% system illustrates a much more favorable profit picture. This method is beginning to find acceptance in a segment of the profession. It enables the designer who cannot compete on a full retail basis—because of geographic and economic factors—to offer some incentive of discount to his clients while still maintaining a fair profit for his services.

The Percentage Off Retail is unquestionably preferable to the Cost-Plus basis.

4. *Flat Fee*

The system of charging a sum for all facets of the designer's services on the job and having the client pay to trade sources and workrooms all charges for merchandise, workmanship, cartage, and other expenses, which they bill directly to him, is based on the theory, summarized at the beginning of this chapter, that all professional people should charge only for their time and skill, and not for tangible goods delivered. This is a perfectly valid theory. And a small percentage of interior designers use the flat-fee system in a small percentage of their work.

But in practice the system is extremely difficult to calculate safely, and very few clients are willing to accept it. Its chief application so far has been in relatively uncomplicated non-residential jobs and in a few very special and unusual residences for extremely sophisticated clients who are absolutely not typical of the public which comprises the market for the vast majority of interior designers in this country.

The flat-fee system appears simple. In fact, it poses a serious financial hazard, since it requires the designer to guess in advance how much time and work he will need to put into the job, calculating his fee to be the cost of that time plus a profit. Once having committed him-

self to a fee, he is bound by the figure. If the job entails more work than he anticipated, he can lose money.

In residential work particularly, it is virtually impossible to project the service and time requirements because of the variables which may develop in the designer-client relationship—the budget, the uncertain temperament of a husband-and-wife client team, the inability of clients to make up their minds about the concepts and items suggested by the designer, and the vagueness of the completion date (since many residential jobs run on a piecemeal basis, with completion one or more years in the future or never).

In cases where the potential client expects or requests the flat-fee method, the designer must not quote a figure without carefully analyzing the following factors as a basis for the calculation:

1. A thorough and detailed understanding of the services to be rendered and the specific areas involved, with the proviso that no additional services and areas are to be added.

2. The client's budget. The budget must be realistic, since the sums a client spends have a direct bearing on the amount of work the designer will be expected to do. The size of the budget has a direct psychological bearing on the size of the fee the designer can quote.

3. The time required to do the job:

a. Design concept time
b. Layouts and specifications
c. Renderings or sketches if required
d. Working drawings—if required

e. Consultation with clients, architects, contractors, etc.

f. Supervision of trades, expediting of orders from sources

g. Shopping time and/or market research

h. Supervising installation

4. A comparison of time spent on prior installations as similar as possible in time factors as the contemplated job is one of the last steps in the calculation. Here is where the designer who has kept job records and has had them systematically analyzed will be in a favorable position to draw valid conclusions about time requirements.

5. Flat Fee Plus Percentage of Costs

Since the client's budget has a definite relationship to the calculation of the flat fee, it is imperative that the designer protect himself against the eventuality of an expansion in the budget while the job is in progress. He can do this by quoting a fee and stipulating in addition that he also receive a percentage of all costs over the original budget. This point is related to remarks on the role of the budget in the preceding paragraphs on the Flat-Fee basis, and to Chapter 11, which is devoted entirely to the subject of the client's budget. To clarify the point sufficiently for this chapter, however, we can give the reader a simple illustration: If the client has set out to spend a total sum of $15,000 —assuming a reasonable $5,000 fee—and later, imagining that he has the designer in his pocket, decides to loosen up and spend $25,000, the designer should not let the original fee stand but insist on negotiating an additional fee calculated as a percentage of the extra expenditure. The percentage may vary from 10% to 25% depending upon the conditions of the ori-

ginal fee and the designer's bargaining position.

6. Hourly and Per-Diem Fees

The time-charge basis for computing a designer's fee is more widely accepted in the non-residential than in the residential field, and even in the non-residential field it is more often used in addition to other fee bases than alone for the computation of the whole fee. For a thorough understanding of time charges, the reader should also study Chapter 23 on the Theory, Objectives, and Methods of Recording Time, and Chapter 18 on Fees and Compensations Specific to the Non-Residential Field. But for the purposes of this chapter, which is to define and compare all the fundamental bases of establishing fees, it is enough to point out that the time-charge is extremely difficult to establish in connection with extensive or complete residential installations. Historically, clients will examine, question, and more often than not disbelieve the amount of time required and used by a designer in the completion of a residential job.

Even with a time record kept with painstaking care by the designer, there is no possible way to record proper compensation when he solves a knotty problem over a cup of coffee, or when a spark of creativeness strikes as he tosses through a sleepless night.

The hourly or per-diem charge is useful, however, in connection with special services rendered by the designer. Examples of services for which these methods of computation are logical, effective, and convenient are:

a. Consultations on specific problems.

59

b. Initial consultations with a prospective client at the client's residence (to cover travel time and brain-picking).

c. Travel to markets and shopping time when the purchases for the clients are minor and the resulting profit mark-up is insufficient to cover the designer's time. Presumably such travel and market research are undertaken at the client's request in search of items specified for special conditions or whims.

d. Services rendered in collaboration with architects or workmen with regard to the construction or alteration of residences.

e. Preparations of specifications and/or working drawings in connection with a specific or isolated problem.

Hourly rates vary considerably with the size of the organization, its overhead and operating costs, and the geographical location. The subject is covered in greater depth in Chapter 23, but again we can summarize here that in those design organizations which maintain a staff, the hourly charge for the time of staff members should not be less than three times the actual payroll cost. The principal's time-charge in such organizations may vary from $30 to $50 or $60 an hour. Comparatively small firms or individual designers have been using a base hourly charge of approximately $25. These figures have been arrived at through official professional conferences and informal discussions among groups of designers. *Our reader would be well advised, however, to avoid using arbitrary figures and to develop their own through analysis of their particular fee requirements in relation to their payroll, overhead costs, competition, the economic conditions*

of their geographical location, and their own availability.

The same considerations must be evaluated in connection with flat per-diem charges. *There must exist a logical relationship between productive time spent and the factors outlined above, and a sensible and realistic value must be placed on the designer's time.*

It should be noted that a designer can often have logical reasons to use more than one fee or compensation base in a single job. The analysis of the job may indicate two or more distinct phases of work. For example:

Assume that the job requires:

1. working with the architect,

2. an expenditure of travel time to major market sources, and

3. completing the design job through the purchasing of all services and furnishings. The designer may well apply the following fee arrangements:

Phase I   —Hourly rate for time spent with architect.
Phase II —Per-Diem rate on travel time.
Phase III —Retail basis for all purchases.

Chapter Ten

Provision for Other Job Cost Factors in Setting Fees

The preceding chapter analyzed several fee and compensation methods which a design firm can use, and in addition indicated that a thorough preliminary analysis of the job is essential to the selection of the most advantageous method or combination of methods.

Before leaving the subject of fees, however, it is necessary to survey a fringe area affecting the income from each job—indirect job cost factors.

Inherent in almost every design job are certain types of costs which, while not relevant to the evaluation of the basis to be chosen for computing the fee, can bite into the designer's margin of profit. Some of these hidden costs are readily exposed if the conditions of a job are carefully thought through at the outset. Others unfortunately come to light too late, and absorb a substantial slice of the profit.

Many of the potential problem areas have been outlined in the discussion of the letter of agreement. If, in addition to taking enough time and trouble to analyze his fee basis, the designer also carefully examines the conditions of the job and the character of his client—viewing them under a microscope, so to speak—the indirect job cost factors may to a great extent become apparent.

Typical indirect job cost factors that crop up often enough to be checked off by the designer as a matter of routine include the following:

A. The Indecisive Client.
The client who cannot make up his mind about the design concept or about specific purchases forces the designer to spend excessive time at the drawing board in revising the design proposals and/or excessive time in shopping. It is, therefore, essential for the designer to evaluate the client's character at the beginning of the job. In a low-budget job with a small profit, such delays can be disastrous. Is the client the wavering type? Can he visualize design proposals? If he cannot—and very few laymen can—is he likely to trust the designer's judgment or must he see everything? If the designer suspects that the client may hem and haw, he can protect himself against excessive hours without compensation in the terms included in the letter of agreement.

B. Conditions Entailing High Delivery Charges.
If the client's premises are on the upper floor of a high-rise building and the designer purchases a piece of furniture too large or too heavy to be delivered on the elevator or stairs, who will be responsible for the hoisting charges? If it cannot be delivered at all, who then will be responsible for the item's cost? The designer must check out the job site for conditions that will prevent easy delivery and installation and he must do this *before* proceeding with orders. If pieces difficult to deliver are to be ordered in any case, the client must be notified in writing indicating his liability for costs and risks entailed in the circumstances of the job site; and, of course, the designer must wait for the client's signed approval before proceeding.

C. Job-Site Conditions Entailing Custom Work.
Physical conditions at the job site are also a frequent cause for custom work, involving such items as air-conditioning vents, radiators, unusually high or unusually low ceilings, etc. If the designer's preliminary review of the job has not revealed all such conditions and taken them into account, he may be forced to bear a costly burden.

D. Custom Design for Special Items.
The amount of custom design in any job de-

pends very much on the designer's creative interest in the design challenge presented, as well as the numberless variables of the client, the budget, and the situation. Whether the custom design is for structural carpentry, special furniture, special fabric treatments, or other objects, works of art, or lighting, the point to bear in mind *in advance* is that a great deal more time at the designer's drawing board will be required. It is not enough to add the cost of workmen's labor and materials to arrive at the base for the mark-up on such items. The creative cost—for the designer's own time and talent —must be accounted for in the charge for the finished piece. Too often the designer fails to take his own contribution into consideration.

E. Costs Created by the Designer's Own Custom Items.

Expenses may develop because of the characteristics of certain things which the designer creates to the client's order, without either the client or the designer anticipating these expenses. The question which then arises is who shall pay these expenses? For example: The job called for and the client wanted a large, custom-built wall unit. The designer worked out the specifications and received a cost estimate from the cabinetmaker. Based upon this estimate, the designer quoted a price to the client which the client accepted. When the unit was finished, the cabinetmaker found that because of its size, it could not be shipped in one piece. It had to be disassembled, shipped, and reassembled on the job site. Since the cabinetmaker was not responsible for estimating the cost of installation, but only the cost of the item, he charged five hundred dollars for his extra work and travel time. The designer then asked the client to reimburse him for these extra five hundred dollars. The client refused, answering that he had

agreed only to the original price quoted by the designer—a price which was to cover the entire cost of the item *installed*, and that he was not required to make good for the designer's mistakes. Actually the designer had made no mistake. He had designed what was wanted. His costly boner lay in failing to consider the problems posed by the specific design and in failing to provide for the extra costs entailed.

It has been said that anticipation is the secret of success. Whether it is the *whole* secret is highly debatable, but in interior design at least, anticipation is certainly one of the prime essentials for success.

F. Costs Entailed by an Unready or Distant Job Site.

In many jobs, the erection of the building and the design and preparation of the interior proceed simultaneously. If the building falls behind schedule, the interior designer, having proceeded with the ordering of furnishings and services, may find that the merchandise is ready for delivery before the premises are in condition to receive them, with the result that the furnishings must be placed in storage—involving extra costs for warehousing and delivery. The designer should check out in advance the possibility of such predicaments, and should advise the client of his liability for such extraordinary costs.

The location of the job may have other effects upon the shipping and installation costs of the job. Many designers who operate from major market centers have learned to solve the problem of a distant job by having all the merchandise assembled in a local storage warehouse, held there until installation time, and then shipped. If this contingency can be anticipated

at the inception of a job, coverage for the costs
involved should be stipulated in the letter of
agreement or confirmations of purchase proposals.

G. Need for Technical or Professional Collaborators.

Early study of the job conditions should indicate whether technical or other professional
assistance will be required. If the job entails
major alterations to the building, for example,
it may be necessary to call in an architect or
licensed engineer. If so, the designer should
watch out for the costs entailed, and provide for
reimbursement by the client. This is especially
important when the designer works on a flat-
fee basis for the complete package. If the designer is not sure at the outset that technical or
professional collaborators will be needed, he
should provide for such contingencies in the
quoted fee or as a separate fee condition.

The problem of indirect job cost factors cannot
be disposed of by any all-inclusive formula.
These factors have a way of becoming apparent
only when the job is well under way. The fact
remains that they do crop up and can cause unnecessary financial losses. They can be kept under control only by the alertness of the designer
in spotting the danger signals before it is too
late to take steps to protect himself.

Chapter Eleven

The Client's Budget

I have repeatedly emphasized the phrase "Scope of Services" in previous chapters dealing with the *letter of agreement* and *fees and compensations*. The client's budget, an integral factor in the scope of services is so important that it requires a special chapter of its own.

In the residential field the client's budget—the sum which he has set aside for the redesign and refurnishing of his house or apartment—is a major factor in the relationship between designer and client and in the satisfactory completion of a job.

It is important to understand first what is meant by the word *budget*. *Budget* is used here to describe the sum available to the designer to be expended for the entire job, including the designer's fee. It is not to be confused with the adjective describing an *insufficiency of funds* that permits only a low-end or inexpensive job, or simply a synonym for the word *inexpensive*. The budget is the sum of money, large or small, which the client expects to spend on the interior.

The budgetary aspects of a proposed interior design job are approached by different clients in different ways:

1. Some clients do not want to set a predetermined figure for the budget. They ask that the designer develop a concept and complete it in all phases of furnishings, services, etc., without any limitation whatsoever as to costs. The average designer may not see this kind of *carte blanche* or price-no-object job once in a lifetime.

2. Some clients approach the designer with the request that he estimate the budget required to carry out a specified design concept. Such clients then react to the quoted budget amount by:

a. fully accepting it, or

b. asking the designer to change the design concept to bring it in line with a lower or higher budget.

3. Some clients tell the designer that they have a specific sum to spend for an interior and ask him to develop a concept within this budget.

4. Some clients work with a designer on the basis of spreading the work out over a period of time as funds become available, doing perhaps a room or small area each time.

The designer must seriously concern himself with the client's budgetary position because of the effect it has upon the client's ability to pay for the designer's development of the job. It is a complete waste of time and effort to attempt to develop a design concept without knowing the budget. Since the number of possibilities for the design and decoration of an interior are limitless, it is impossible to "come up right" without some preliminary idea of what the client wants —and what he wants to spend is a major factor in what he wants.

Effect of the Budget on the Fee Basis

The size of the budget is of great importance to the designer in the selection of a proper fee or compensation base, because it enables the designer to estimate the direct and indirect costs of the job and the profit to be earned. This potential profit is then related to the work involved, and the designer can make his decision as to whether to take the job or not, and if he takes it, on what fee basis.

For example: If the designer has a $50,000 budget and the job is on the retail basis, he can quickly come to the realization that the gross profit resulting from this job should be approximately $15,000 to $17,500. This profit should normally cover concept time, design time, and job development time.

If, on the other hand, the budget is only $5,000, the resulting profit will probably be only $1,200 to $1,500. Now the designer will have to analyze the time to be spent in relation to earning the small amount indicated. He may very well come to the conclusion that:

1. he cannot take the job;

2. he should require a design fee or some other additional payment (these have previously been discussed under fees and compensations) along with the retail mark-up.

The budget has a direct psychological relation to the size of a quotable fee if the job calls for a flat-fee base. To illustrate:

If a budget is $25,000, and the designer requests a flat fee of $5,000 for his work, the relationship of fee to the total amount to be spent is more apt to be viewed by the potential client as being within reason than if the budget is $5,000 and the designer's fee is quoted at $2,000. This fee of $2,000 might be quite proper because of the work involved for the designer, and yet the client is more apt to balk at the fee because it appears to have an outlandish relationship to the total budget.

Observance of the Client's Budget
Once the designer has determined the client's anticipated budget, he must analyze the job requirements. The budget must be realistic in relation to the scope of services and to the furnishings the client desires. Preliminary budget estimates must be prepared (Chapter 12) and checked against the required budget.

If this analysis discloses that, based upon the designer's concept and the client's desires, the job cannot be brought in within the framework of the client's budget, then the designer is faced with the following alternatives:

1. to revise the design concept and furnishing schedule.
2. to advise the client that the particular concept must be changed unless the client desires to review and increase the budget.
3. If, within the esthetic and quality requirements of the job, the designer cannot change the concept and the furnishing or the construction schedules, and the client refuses to increase the budget, then the designer should drop the job before starting.

The designer has absolutely no right to spend one dollar more of a client's money than the client will authorize him to spend. Some clients, once advised that the budget might be tight, will instruct the designer to go ahead and they will be responsible for additional required funds as long as they approve each purchase. Other clients will be adamant that a budget be adhered to. The actual experience of a successful design firm is summarized:

The client purchased a very large and expensive co-op apartment. He gave the designer a budget of $60,000 and "not one dollar more." The designer recognized that the apartment could not possibly be furnished in the manner the client wanted for this amount. Rather than do a very bad job or, to be more accurate, an impossible job, the designer refused the work. It is significant that the designer who eventually did take the job wound up in a legal controversy with the client. It takes courage and wisdom to turn down a job, but when need be, do so. The worst possible thing a designer can do is to proceed with a job, wishfully hoping that he can bring it home within the budget, but that if he fails, the client will come up with more money.

Failure to work within a client's budget can cause financial losses in many ways, such as the following:

1. Accounts receivable balances due from the client may be completely uncollectible or at best collectible over a long period of time.
2. The designer may have to accept the return of some of the furnishings and accessories, and, since so much of a designer's work is custom, may find it difficult or impossible to dispose of it, so that the possibility of recouping costs is negligible.
3. In order to finish the job, the designer may be forced to give the client unwarranted adjustments and allowances.
4. The designer and the client may easily become involved in costly lawsuits.
5. Damage to a designer's reputation when he becomes involved in situations of this kind can be most harmful to his future.

Chapter Twelve

Estimation and Control of the Budget

To develop a client's budget requirements for a job, or conversely, to the design for a job to meet a specific budget, requires thoughtful planning and the recording of the results of such planning in a methodical manner. This can be accomplished only by the use of proper control methods.

The control must reflect all the information needed for the client's guidance as to cost, and for the designer's guidance as to development of the job:

1. Preliminary plans and layouts.
2. Listing of anticipated items of furnishings and services to be purchased.
3. Estimated costs to be incurred.
4. Estimated selling prices to the client.
5. Comparison of actual prices to estimated prices.
6. Final disposition of estimated lists of items to be considered.

Exhibit A—"Designer's Work Sheet for Budget Estimate Control"—sets up the necessary control and manages the flow of required information in a routine and well-defined manner. It relates and ties in the required information outlined above. The ideal system for the best use of this form is outlined below. It requires a great deal of paper work, but despite the objections that have been raised against paper work, the results are well worth the effort and time invested.

Step One—Preliminary Plans and Layouts:
The designer should prepare preliminary floor plans and room layouts as the very first step in arriving at his design concept. After the preparation and study of a few arrangements, the designer selects the layout he is most likely to use. On the floor plan he indicates the various pieces of furniture and accessories to be used and their position in the room. Each item indicated on the room plan is marked with a number. Duplicate pieces of fur-

nishings such as "a pair of commodes" bear the same number, as indicated on Exhibit "B" as item (1). Actually, examination of the floor plan will indicate a complete scale drawing of room size and furnishings, including the draperies (23) and chandelier (2).

Step Two—"Designer's Work Sheet":
After the floor plan has been laid out and furnishing requirements have been firmed up in the designer's mind, Exhibit A is prepared. Since at this point the designer is seeking basically an estimate work-up, it is not necessary to complete all the information reflected by the columnar headings.

Referring to the floor plan, the designer now begins to insert the information called for on Exhibit A as follows:

Column (1)—The article of furnishing as coded on the room layout.

Column (2)—The number of pieces of the same article.

Column (5)—Identification of the article, such as bed, table, chair, etc.

Columns (7), (8), (9)—The designer now allocates the estimated cost and subsequent estimated billing price to the client for each intended item of furnishing.

At this point it is important to note that there may be items to be entered on the work sheet (Exhibit A) which may not appear on the floor plans, such as painting, alterations, carpeting, etc. The work sheet (Exhbit A) must always reflect additional costs or services for any item reflected on the floor plan, i.e. .... draperies would reflect a line for the

A

Designer's Work Sheet for Budget Estimate Control Company Name											Client: *John Jones* Area *Drawing Rm/Gallery*	
			Description			Estimated Cost		Estimated Selling Price	Actual Cost	Actual Selling Price	Purchased	
Item No.	Quan.	Source	Mfr. #	Item	Color or Finish	Per Unit	Total				Date	Purchase Order No.
①	②	③	④	⑤	⑥	⑦	⑧	⑨	⑩	⑪	⑫	⑬

Form No. 5   (To obtain forms, see page 10.)

A 1

Designer's Work Sheet for Budget Estimate Control
Company Name

Client: John Jones
Area: Drawing Rm/Gallery

Item No.	Quan.	Source	Description			Estimated Cost		Estimated Selling Price	Actual Cost	Actual Selling Price	Purchased	
			Mfr. #	Item	Color or Finish	Per Unit	Total				Date	Purchase Order No.
1	2	Designer–Inv.	F 2529	Consoles		450-	900-	1400-	900-	1400-	11/10	7114
2	1	ABC Antiques		Chand.	Bronze		300-	500-	400-	666	11/11	7119
16	1	Hoffstater Furn	1235	Sofa (in muslin)			600-	900 -	600 -	900-	11/14	7231
16	18 yds	XYZ Fabric Co.	X 324	Fabric for sofa	9⁰⁰ yd	162-	216 -	162-	216-	11/14	7232
16	9 yds	HS Trimming Co.	H 926	Braid for sofa	12-yd	108-	162-	108-	162-	11/14	7233
17	1	Paul Jones	FN 396P	Coffee Table 48x29 glass top		360	600 -	360-	600-	11/17	7290
23		Drapery Mfg Co.		1 pair curtains		200-	250 —	300-	375—		
23	32 yds	XYZ Fabric Co.	To 2057	Curtain material white	3⁰⁰	96	125 —	128-	212-		

B

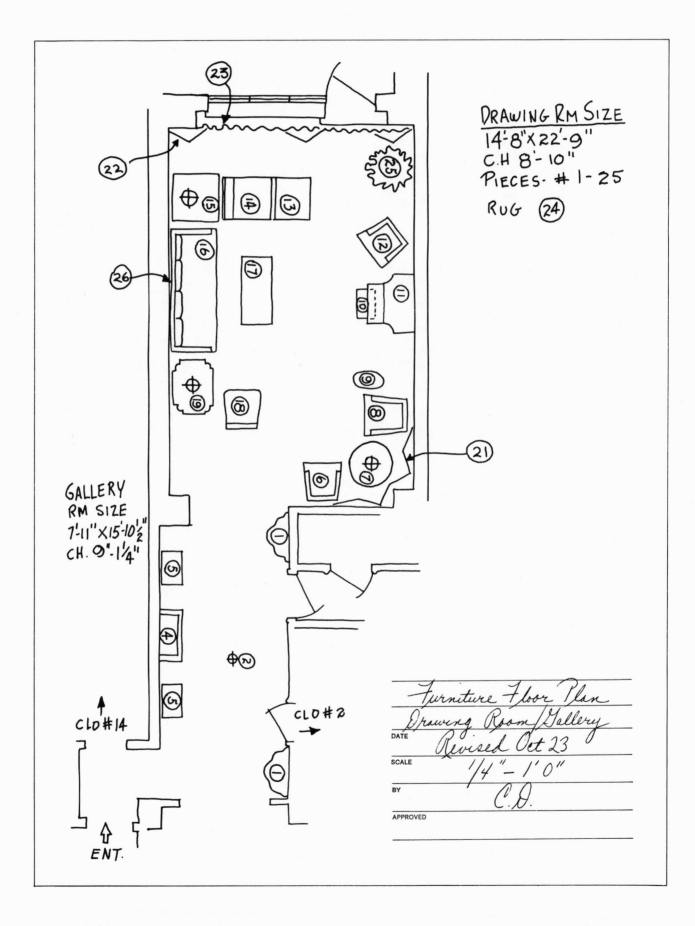

DRAWING RM SIZE
14'-8" X 22'-9"
C.H 8'-10"
PIECES. # 1-25
RUG ㉔

GALLERY
RM SIZE
7'-11" X 15'-10½"
CH. 9"-1¼"

CLO #14

CLO #2

ENT.

Furniture Floor Plan
Drawing Room/Gallery
DATE Revised Oct 23
SCALE ¼" – 1'0"
BY C.D.
APPROVED

fabric identification and cost; a line for workshop identification and cost; and possibly a line for trimming identification and cost.

Eventually this work sheet, properly prepared, enables the designer to total the estimated cost column and estimated selling price column and arrive at an estimated budget figure that ties into the design concept. All of this information can now be used for discussions with the client towards the establishment of the budget for a specific design concept on a sound basis, backed up by a decent working memorandum.

As discussions about the budget proceed between the designer and the client, changes will usually have to be made on this preliminary work-up. All that is necessary for the designer to do is:

1. If the estimated expenditure for a particular item of furnishing is to be changed, simply to substitute the information called for in columns (7), (8), (9).
2. If a listed item is to be replaced, simply to draw a line through the item to be substituted and enter the new item on the next empty line.

In preparing this preliminary budget work-up, the designer may find it of great assistance to note the source information—columns (3), (4) and (6),

1. as a guide for establishing the source of the costs of items of furnishings,
2. as a guide for discussions with clients by indicating a picture, or sample of a specific item,
3. as a base from which to prepare the final control sheet from which the actual job is controlled.

It should be evident to the reader that the preliminary work-up as described herein is simple and effective in preparing the flow of information necessary:

1. To prepare a budget estimate where the potential client has a request for the design and decoration of his residence without any concept as to its cost. His requirements are such that he will not proceed with a job *until he knows where he is going from a financial standpoint.*

2. To prepare a design concept and furnishing schedule where the potential client has a definite and firm budget with which to work. This preliminary work-up enables the designer to see *how far he can go* with the amount allocated by the client for the project.

Once this first phase of estimated budget and design concept has been firmed up and finalized between the client and the designer, the designer will find that this budget control form (Exhibit A) will be invaluable in controlling the flow of work.

If only a few changes have been made in the preliminary budget work sheets, then these can be used without redoing new work sheets for the progress control of the job. If many changes have been made and if the preliminary floor plan has been extensively changed, *then the designer must start with a clean work-up program for control.*

Budget-estimate control and work-flow control is illustrated by recording on Exhibit A-1 the following selected items indicated on "Furniture Floor Plan—**Exhibit B**."

Item 1—A pair of consoles owned as inventory by the designer. It is to be noted that the estimated costs are the same as the actual cost and selling price, since the designer owned these pieces and was certain of the prices.

Item 2—An antique chandelier is to be used, and only an estimate of the amount to be spent could be indicated, since the actual accessory had to be located first. Here, the actual selling price is higher than the estimate given; therefore, the designer is aware that he is exceeding the budget. As the job progresses he is now aware of "overage" and "underage" of the actual sum to be spent as compared to the estimate.

Item 16—A sofa to be covered in selected fabric and selected braid. Here, the control form indicates the firm that is making the sofa and the necessity of selecting and purchasing the fabric required for covering and the braid required as trim.

Item 17—A coffee table selected from a specific manufacturer's regular line, complete and with no change in the quoted price.

Item 23—Curtains to be made by a workshop from selected fabric. Here the designer, in his original estimate, set aside a budget figure. However, when actual specifications were drawn, the cost was higher and here again it was necessary for the designer to be aware of the change as it affects the budget. It is to be noted that this example points out the care that is needed in listing the items to be budgeted and purchased where the item called for requires a combination of sources for completion.

At any point the designer has immediately available to him a comparison of his estimated budget amounts, both cost price and selling price, to the actual cost and the necessary marked-up selling price. If the information indicates potential problems with the client because of price changes and their resulting effect on budget, or if the analysis indicates a lack of profit margin for the designer, then the time to make changes is before the purchase orders are sent out.

The last two columns of the budget estimate form indicate the status of the contemplated purchases of material and services for the area involved. If columns (12) and (13) are blank, it will indicate that "no action" has been taken. In this manner the designer is constantly informed as to what has been ordered, what has not been ordered, and what further work must be done.

Variations of "estimate control forms" can be adapted to suit the needs and requirements of individual design firms, depending upon their size, staff, and type of clientele.

Form—Exhibit C is good because it sets up a control where more than one service is to be performed for a specific item, i.e., draperies are to be made of special-order fabric that has to be bought.

Column (1)—item number from plan.

Columns (2), (3)—identifies the drapery workshop.

Columns (5), (6), (7), (8)—identifies the fabric of which the draperies are to be made.

Thus, with this type of form, there is less possibility of omitting items to be included in the budget.

Form—Exhibit D is a combination of budget control and delivery control. Here it is possible to maintain control of items to be purchased in accordance with the budget, with adherance to budgetary requirements indicated through an analysis of the last four columns. In addition, when merchandise and services are ordered, control is maintained as to their status in the hands of a supplier.

C

Estimate Control Form
Company Name

Residence of

Room

Plan No.	Quantity	Item and No.	Firm	Yardage	Fabric No.	Color	Firm	Finish	P. O. No.
①	②	③	④	⑤	⑥	⑦	⑧	⑨	⑩
23	1 pr.	Curtains	Drapery Mfg.	32	TO 2057	White	XYZ Fabric		

Form No. 6   (To obtain forms, see page 10.)

D

Budget Delivery Control
Company Name

Date: Client: Cost

Room					Date		Promised	Actual	Budget		Actual	
	Amounts		Description & Source	Expedite	Ordered	Checked	Delivery	Delivery	Wholesale	Retail	Wholesale	Retail
1												
2												
3												
4												
5												
6												
7												
8												
9												
10												
11												
12												
13												
14												
15												
16												
17												
18												
19												
20												
21												
22												

Form No. 7   (To obtain forms, see page 10.)

Chapter Thirteen

Purchase Orders

After the first phase of a design job has been set up—in other words, after the completion of the planning, design concept, and furnishing schedules —it becomes necessary to begin ordering the necessary services and material furnishings from trade sources and work shops.

A designer need but envision the multiplicity of items and services that must be coordinated, ordered, followed up at the source level, and installed, to realize the mistakes and costly problems that can result if a planned method of purchase control is not observed.

It must be a definite practice in any design firm, regardless of size (including a one-man operation), that no tangible item or service should ever be ordered for a client without the use of a written purchase order.

It is essential to understand that properly executed purchase orders are vital instruments in connection with:

A. The design firm's relationship with trade sources, its supervision and control to assure the proper completion of all orders it has placed, and
B. The maintenance of an internal office procedure to correlate the buying and services required for a job with the basic design program, the eventual completion of orders by sources, and the design firm's billing to the client.

A. Relationship with Trade Sources
Improper ordering of merchandise by designers account for a major source of irritation between design firms and trade sources. Errors in designating or describing purchases to be made are a costly expense factor which each designer bears, since purchasing is his responsibility.

However, a properly prepared purchase order, complete in all details, and containing a full description of the purchase to be made or the service to be performed, will cut down on the probability of errors. It places the responsibility for proper execution of the order in the hands of the trade sources. This is especially important in the design field because so much which designers order are special in size, construction, finish, etc.

The preparation of any purchase order and the information it may contain varies somewhat with the special requirements of the work done by the design firm. Samples of actual purchase order forms used by two interior design organizations reproduced here are functional, and can be used as a guide in determining the format suitable for any given design office.

The purchase order form marked Exhibit A contains all information which would be pertinent to placing an order in a clear and concise manner:

1. Pre-printed numbers—important for control and identification.

2. Name and address of supplier.

3. Date order has been placed.

4. "Deliver to" instruction—most important because deliveries can be made either to a client's premises or to other trade sources for additional work. For example, a fabric house needs to know to what workshop the fabric should be sent to be made into draperies. Deliveries may also be made to warehouses for storage before the installation. It is of utmost importance that a source know where to deliver an item so as to

Company Name   **Purchase Order**
Address
                                      No. 0000

                                      This Order Number must appear on your invoice and package

_____   196

_____

_____

Please enter our order for goods named below:

_____

Deliver to:

Tag For: Job No.   When Ship: Ship Via:

Quantity   Description   Price   Per   Extension

Price must not be higher than last charged.   **Company Name**
Acknowledge order and state when you will ship.

Rec'd   Checked   Posted   Approved by

A

Form No. 8   (To obtain forms, see page 10.)

avoid unnecessary freight charges or losses of the merchandise.

5. Tag for – this information identifies the client for whom the purchase is being made and the purpose of the purchase. For example, fabric purchased from a fabric house to be sent to a workshop for the making of living room draperies would read: *client's name/Lv. Rm. draperies*. Thus, when the workshop receives a packaged parcel of fabrics, the shipping tag will immediately identify its contents.

6. Job number—used as further identification if a job number system is used by the firm.

7. Shipping date—advises the supplier as to when the goods should be shipped, depending upon the installation date or the designer's need for the merchandise.

8. Shipping instructions—indicates a designer's preference for shipping methods or carriers to be used, depending upon cost, geography, and time requirements, etc.

9. Specification of goods ordered, quantity, and price—this area of information is, of course, the vital one in spelling out completely the identification and description of the proposed purchase. The description should be clear and detailed, placing the burden of proper delivery on the source. It is correct practice to attach cuttings, strike-offs, samples, specifications, etc., to the purchase orders for additional information.

In order to indicate a clear, concise statement of services or goods to be ordered and their costs, it may be necessary to obtain estimates from various sources. Estimates should be obtained before issuing purchase orders involving custom work and contractors' services, e.g. carpentry, painting, alterations, etc.

The consistent preparation of purchase orders following the format outlined above cuts down costly errors and enables design firms to maintain good rapport with trade sources.

B. Internal Office Procedures and the Control of Purchasing

The consistent use of purchase orders affords the design organization the soundest base for the control of simultaneous ordering for any number of jobs in progress. The purchase order is the relating factor integral to the internal procedure of a design office because:

1. It relates to the basic floor plans and furnishing schedules of each job, and controls the ordering of goods as described in Chapter 12.

2. It maintains a record of all outstanding orders placed with sources.

3. It maintains a record for the checking of bills charged by the vendors, and identifies the merchandise charged for.

4. It serves as a control basis for eventual billing to the client.

Purchase orders should be prepared in triplicate as a minimum. The use of more than three copies would depend on the requirements of each particular interior design organization and its own procedural format. The larger the office, the more copies may be required.

Procedure for the small design office: Three copies are prepared and used in the following manner:

a. First copy—white—for vendor.
b. Second copy—pink—for "open purchase order file."
c. Third copy—yellow—for client's folder.

A. *Vendor's copy, white,* is forwarded to the trade source.

B. *"Open Purchase Order File" copy, pink*—It is of utmost importance for a design firm to know at all times the status of orders that have been placed, not only for each individual job but for an overall picture of the current status of the firm's work. Therefore, a copy of every purchase order written should be filed in numerical sequence in a readily accessible binder. This binder will now constitute a base to which the designer will refer to frequently to check on undelivered orders. Constant review of this "open purchase order file" will refresh the designer's memory as to the status of his jobs and alert him to possible problems with regard to meeting delivery and installation dates.

The "open purchase order file" is kept current, because as goods and services are delivered by the sources and invoices are rendered to the design office, the purchase orders are extracted from the file and matched to the supplier's invoice. They are compared for quantity, description, and price.

In the small design office, especially the one-man organization, this copy of the purchase order that has been extracted from the open file can play another role besides the one described above. This copy, after having been checked against the supplier's invoice, can be used as a master copy for billing purposes. The copy of the purchase order is checked for correctness and placed in a folder marked: "to be billed to clients." When the client is to be billed, the purchase order is removed from the "to be billed" folder and the billing date and invoice number are added to it. This method of billing control is simple and not too time-consuming. However, the fact that control is based on loose sheets of paper could defeat the control base for billing if these copies of the purchase orders are misplaced in any fashion.

C. *Client's Folder copy, yellow*—The third copy of the purchase order is placed in the client's folder or file for ready reference.

Procedure in Larger Design Firms: In the larger design firm the same procedure can be used, but it may require additional copies, depending upon how the information is to be routed.

A typical procedure for a larger firm can be illustrated using the purchase order form marked Exhibit B. This is a six-copy form with white, pink, yellow, and three green copies. The designer placing the order handwrites the necessary information on an inter-office "Requisition for Purchase Order" and sends this "Requisition" to the front office for typing. The order clerk maintains the numerical sequence since "Requisitions" will come from more than one designer.

a. *White copy* goes to vendor. (Note that the white copy is a shorter form than the other copies, since the vendor's copy records only the cost price and the other copies record cost prices and billing price to client.)

b. *Pink copy* is returned to the designer together with the original "Requisition for P.O.," so that the designer can check for error and

B

Client		**Purchase Order Number**	
Room			
Used For		Date	
		Due	
		Ship to	
Company Name			
Address			
To		Bill to	
Attn:	Tel.		

Quantity	Details	Unit	Price		Unit	Charge

All merchandise must be shipped prepaid   Approved by
Order number and name of client must appear on invoices
If prices are incorrect or order cannot be filled exactly as above, advise immediately

Form No. 9   (To obtain forms, see page 10.)

maintain for himself a continuing record of the ordering for each particular job.

c. *Yellow copy* is sent to the bookkeeping department for entry in "Vendor's Open Purchase Order File."

d. *Green copy* is also sent to bookkeeping department for entry in "Client's Open Purchase Order File." This is the file which controls billing to the client.

The extra green copies are prepared when required for any special purpose. For example, if the item to be purchased is to be billed direct to the client, these extra copies are available to be sent to the client as his record of purchases made by the design office, and are used as his check against invoices he will receive from trade sources.

Chapter Fourteen

Client's Inventory and Billing Control

In the natural sequence of steps in estimating the costs of a job, the preparation of purchasing schedules and the preparation of purchase orders is followed by the orderly control of the actual purchases and the eventual billing to the client.

Chapter 12 on *Estimation and Control of the Budget* described the methods by which the designer made an orderly approach to listing the items which should be purchased for the client and the estimated costs of each. It was further indicated that by use of a proper form set-up (Exhibit A—Chapter 12) the actual ordering of the merchandise could be controlled by filling information into two of the columns—the Purchase Order number and date.

Since it is obvious that the original budget estimate form is bound to undergo changes as a result of substitutions before the final selection is made, the use of this form for keeping inventory and for billing control to clients may not work efficiently for all design firms. Some firms may find that the methods and forms described in Chapter 12 are burdensome and unnecessary, because neither their clients nor their work calls for such extensive preliminary layouts.

However, every design office engaged in the purchasing of goods and services for a client must have a ready record of orders placed for the individual client and must at the same time provide a control that will safeguard the eventual billing of such purchases to the client.

There is no more important factor in a design office than being assured that the client is being billed properly for every item purchased for his particular job. It is obvious that if a designer makes a purchase for a client, the designer must pay the source, and if the information pertaining to this purchase is overlooked, lost or forgotten when it is time to charge the client, the designer loses the cost of that item plus his profit. How many mistakes of this type can a design organization make without being seriously affected financially?

Towards the effective control of this phase of a design organization's operations, it is suggested that the following method be considered. The reader should note that the forms described need not be followed blindly, but that they are adaptable to the needs, circumstances, and office procedures of each particular design office.

Exhibit A—Envelope Form

The envelope form serves many purposes and is best suited to the smaller design office. It enables the designer to maintain a constantly available cohesive package of all correspondence, estimates, contracts, copies of purchase orders, samples, pictures, and a visible, easily prepared accounting control and cost record.

To serve its purpose as a control, the envelope form must as a matter of routine be handled with absolute precision. It is based completely on the theory of the preparation of a purchase order for every single item purchased or expended on behalf of the client. The form is printed on both sides of an expansion folder, and, if the job is an extensive one, a separate folder should be used for each area of the installation. The columnar set-up is as follows:

1. Date
2. Purchase order number
3. Dealer
4. Item
5. Cost
6. Freight, etc.
7. Purchase Invoice Received
8. Resale

A

Date	Order Number	Dealer	Item	Cost	P.P.-Ins. Freight	Sundries	Resale	Invoice Number Date	Payment Received Date	Remarks
①	②	③	④	⑤	⑥	⑦	⑧	⑨	⑩	⑪

Client _____

Address _____

Form No. 10 (To obtain forms, see page 10.)

9. Invoice number and date
10. Payment received and date
11. Remarks

The entries on the folder are made from the copy of the prepared purchase order and handled as follows:

The information to be recorded in columns 1 through 5 is taken directly from each purchase order:

1. The date of the purchase order.
2. The number of the purchase order.
3. The name of the vendor to whom the purchase order is addressed.
4. A short identifying description of the item ordered.
5. The cost of the item to the designer.

As these entries are recorded for each prepared purchase order, the designer has a continuing visual listing of goods ordered for the client.

In due time, as the various vendors complete their work and deliver in accordance with instructions, the designer will begin to receive bills from the vendors indicating such delivery and the amount due to them. After the invoice is received and checked against the *open purchase order file* (as described in Chapter 13) the control envelope form is marked with a red check (√) mark in column 7. This now indicates delivery or completion of the specific item. At the same time any freight or delivery charges are entered at column 6 so that these costs can be picked up if they are to be charged to the client.

With continuing review of the client's folder, the designer is constantly aware of the status of the job. He knows what he has ordered for the client, whether the item has been delivered and billed to him by the vendor, and the fact that he has not invoiced his client because columns 8 and 9 have not been noted. As the designer is ready to bill the client, the invoice number and the date of the invoice addressed to the client are entered in column 9, and the price charged to the client is entered in column 8. It should be noted that many designers using this system enter the selling price to the client at the same time that they are entering the first recording step—columns 1 through 5. This gives them immediate control and a record of the price to be charged, without having to recheck for this information later.

Once having completed entries in all columns from 1 through 9, the designer is assured of having billed the client for every item he has ordered.

An open, unentered space in a column will indicate either failure on the part of a source to deliver and/or failure on the part of a designer to charge the client. To restate, if the system is carried through without varying from the base premise that a purchase order be written for every item for a client, and if these purchase orders are entered as described herein, the designer has complete control of his job.

Column 10—Payment received and date can be used by design organizations for various purposes:

1. The small design firm can use the recording of the monies received from clients as a complete accounting record. The folder will indicate in the "Resale" column the amount billed to a client, and if a running total is kept of this column and compared to the running total of monies received, the accounts receivable balance will be quickly pointed out to the designer.

B

Inventory Sheet

Client

Date	Order No.	Dealer	Item	Cost	Resale	Invoice No. and Date	Payment Rec'd and Date	Remarks

Form No. 11 (To obtain forms, see page 10.)

C

Job Control

For: _____ Designer _____ Job No. _____ Page ____ of ____

Proposal ☐   Acknowledgment ☐   Special Instructions: _____ Client: _____

Est. Date: _____ Street: _____

Contract Date: _____ City & State: _____

Contract Rec'd: _____ Att'n: _____

Item No.	Supplier and Shipping Instructions	Q'ty	Supplier's Number	Description Size, Color, Finish, Etc.	Cost A/C	List/Selling Price		%	Cost		P.O. No.	Del. Date
						Each	Total		Each	Total		

2. Column 10 can be used as a "deposit" reminder against each item. Some design firms use this column to indicate to them the amount of deposit received from the client prior to the time of ordering. (See Chapter 8 regarding deposits received from clients with signed confirmations.)

3. Some design firms use the information recorded in this column as a guide to slow the pace of their placement of orders. If it is evident that many items involving considerable expenditure have been made on behalf of the client (columns 1 through 5) and very little money has been received, the designer may find it prudent to slow down a bit until the client catches up on payments (as discussed in Chapter 15.)

Column 11—Remarks, gives the designer recording space for any comments or notes. Many design firms use this space to record a running total of time spent on the job. This information can be most valuable if the designer will take the time occasionally to compare the running totals of the cost column with the selling price column—and compare the resulting gross profit to the number of hours consumed.

The use of the system described will not only afford control, but if carried out to the completion of each job, will provide excellent statistical information for guidance on estimating the costs and profit potential of future jobs.

At the conclusion of a job, if the Cost column (5), Freight, etc. (6), and Resale (8) are totaled and the total costs subtracted from the total resale amount, the profit figure for the job is immediately derived. This profit figure can be analyzed as to whether the gross profit percentage is proper. If it is not, the incorrect percentage indicates a major error somewhere along the line.

The job profit can be compared to the number of hours expended to determine the hourly or daily rate earned. This becomes an important source or guidance information in:

1. Quoting for future jobs of a similar nature.
2. Review of fee or compensation base if the financial return is too small.
3. Guidance as to the effectiveness of the working methods and habits of staff members.
4. Compilation of these factors over a number of various types of jobs will indicate the areas in which the design office is most effective or least effective.

Exhibit B—Inventory Sheet

In large organizations, the envelope form may not be usable, since a flow of information and data must be channeled between the executive section, the bookkeeping section, and the production or design section. Therefore, the envelope form has been reduced to a form that can be placed in a binder—(Exhibit B).

In the larger organizaton, an adaptation of this form and control is an absolute must. The designer or design department maintains its control by adopting the job control procedures described in Chapter 12 and the flow of financial information is controlled by the bookkeeping department. The control by the bookkeeping department is maintained by the flow of purchase order information. If the designer routes purchase requisition forms to the bookkeeping office and the bookkeeping office actually prepares the purchase order for distribution to the trade source, control is maintained as described under the *Envelope Form.* As long as some office routine is developed so that the bookkeeping department has effective control over purchase orders, the inventorying and billing to clients can be effectively maintained.

Some small design firms find the inventory sheet more desirable than the envelope, since the financial information contained in these forms will not be disclosed every time the designer works with the contents of the envelope. In other words, the client's folder of samples, plans, drawings, contracts, and confirmations can be taken to a client's home for conference purposes, or the contents of the folder can be used for reference when working with contractors, but the fianncial records—cost, selling price, payments, etc.—are left intact in the office and its contents and information remain private.

Exhibit C—Job Control Form
Exhibit C is a sophisticated job control form which is in use in a large interior design firm. It indicates the degree of control that can be worked out, depending upon the needs of any particular organization.

Chapter Fifteen

Billing and Collecting

The final steps in completing the business phase of an interior design installation are properly billing the client for all services rendered and all merchandise purchased for the job, and collecting the money due. In the language of accounting the terms for this are: "billing to clients," and "accounts receivable collections."

It is the writer's opinion that the balance of monies due from a client for delivered goods and services is a most important barometer to watch. The client may have gone overboard, spending more money than he can afford, or he may enthusiastically have made changes with the designer beyond the scope of the original budget. As the job proceeds along various stages to completion, the designer becomes more and more deeply indebted to trade sources. If the designer does not receive funds from the client in payment of delivered items and blithely goes on delivering to the client, his liability to the trades increases, and if it is unchecked, can cause him serious financial distress. It is, therefore, necessary to pay attention to a billing program and to carefully observe its results as the job proceeds.

Each design organization should select a billing program suited to its own ability to organize office routine, and should coordinate this program to the letter of agreement.

Invoices should be prepared in duplicate at least. (Examples of invoice forms are included in Chapter 26 on "Other Working Forms"; refer to Section G.) One copy is mailed to the client and the second copy is retained in the office as part of the bookkeeping records. Many offices prepare sales invoices in triplicate, using one copy to be mailed to the client, one copy for bookkeeping purposes, and one copy for the client's work folder as a ready reference for the designer working on the job. All invoices should be prenumbered so that bookkeep-ing control may be maintained.

Time of Billing

When should a client be billed? To answer this question it is necessary to examine the many facets involved in the pros and cons of the following billing methods:

A. **Billing the client as each item is ready** is probably the most time-consuming system from a viewpoint of paper work. However, it affords the following continuing control for the designer:

1. The inventory control sheet for the client is kept current indicating the actual status of each item.

2. The designer is constantly aware of the amount of money due from the client. As the designer invoices the client, the accounts receivable balance increases until payment is noted, reducing this balance.

3. If the accounts receivable balance due from the client is not reduced but increases constantly, then, at the conclusion of the job, the designer will not be taken unaware by the danger of collection difficulties.

4. At any point the designer, becoming aware of the danger of collection problems, can discreetly begin to hold back his purchase orders and the delivery of goods and services until the client comes to a more current financial position.

5. As far as the client is concerned, constant billing advice is excellent, because it keeps him aware of what he is spending and where he is going. This type of information is invaluable if both the designer and client are aware of finances and if the client has the intention of proceeding with the various phases of a job in accordance with his ability to pay.

6. While this constant flow of billing has many

advantages, its disadvantage lies in the amount of paper work entailed. Office time must be found practically every day for the preparation of the invoices.

B. **Specific Billing Periods**—Many offices set aside a specific day or days of the month (such as the first, the first and the fifteenth, or the last) as *billing day*.

1. If billing is done, for example, on the first and fifteenth of the month, the office work can be routinized to set these days apart for it.
2. Twice a month may be frequent enough, if good control is maintained, to govern and observe the expenditure of funds on the client's behalf.
3. Billing once a month may allow too much of a time lapse to properly observe and safely control the client's account receivable. It can allow a potentially dangerous situation to get out of hand.

C. **Alternative Methods**—Some design firms do not depend on the billing methods so far described as a control factor, but use the following systems for watching what a client owes the designer:

1. The designer requests a major portion of the estimated budget as a fund, and then draws upon this fund as expenditures are made. For example: If the client is spending approximately $10,000, the designer may ask for a $5,000 deposit at the inception of the job. As the designer finds he is incurring purchases approximating the $5,000 deposit, he will ask for more money from the client, at all times working within the funds advanced by the client. Needless to say that this is a most satisfactory arrangement when it is possible. There is resistance on the part of clients in many geo-graphic areas and economic strata to this arrangement, and they simply will not give designers large deposits in advance of ordering.
2. Some designers attempt to have the client pay the trade source directly, but this is often totally unsatisfactory since most sources will not sell directly to the consumer. The ensuing confusion in the routine paper work is hardly worth the effort. If the designer feels that collection may be a problem, the way to overcome that situation is not to have the client pay directly to the source, but for the designer to bill the client in full before purchase is made (pro forma) and wait until the client's check clears the bank before ordering.
3. Many designers compute the total budget at the beginning of the job, advising the client that the payment method is one-third of the budget as a deposit, one-third payable as the major portion of the ordering has been processed, and one-third upon delivery or installation. These terms are set forth in the letter of agreement. The designer keeps the client informed as to the expenditure of the funds by sending him confirmations or statements. This method has its drawback in the last payment. When is a job completed or finally installed? A technically minded or rough client can hold up the final one-third balance until everything is "just right." This arrangement should be used with caution, especially if the final payment is based upon the phrase—"due upon completion of the job."

Credit Terms with Clients

Unlike most entrepreneurs, the interior designer does not require a large amount of capital to start his business and, as a result, may not have sufficient funds to enable him to carry his clients' accounts for a protracted period without endangering his trade credit and standing. Therefore, it becomes necessary to maintain a proper relationship between client and designer assuring that credit terms set by the designer are observed by the client. The designer who is not paid promptly by his clients cannot pay his own bills promptly. A designer who does not promptly pay his bills to his sources will soon find that many good sources will close their doors to him or place him on a *pro forma* or C.O.D. basis. In the face of these stringent trade conditions the designer cannot stay in business unless he in turn enforces stringent payment requirements upon all of his clients. These stringent credit terms in turn will alienate many potential clients.

For example, if a designer has poor credit standing with the sources and must pay on a C.O.D. or *pro forma* basis, he must then request that the client pay in full long before delivery; most clients are loath to do so.

Therefore, a designer should determine, based upon how much capital he has in his firm, what credit terms he will extend to his clients. Once having established these terms, he must enforce them as positively as possible. Basically, if the designer follows the system of demanding deposits before ordering goods, half the battle is won. The other half is to apply credit terms and to make them stick, on one of the following bases:

a. Balance due upon notice of completion by trade source.
b. Balance due upon delivery to the client's premises or warehouse.
c. Balance due in ten days after invoice is rendered. This will assure the designer a smooth flow of funds to use in carrying on normal relations with the trade.

With very few exceptions, almost every design organization has experienced the frustrations of not being able to collect promptly from clients, and many have undergone the unhappy experience of being forced to turn the matter over to attorneys for legal action. The problem of collection is a most troublesome one, and cannot be swept under the carpet. It is the writer's opinion, based upon experience, that when these conditions arise they do so because the designer:

a. Is unaware of dangerous situations until it is too late.
b. If aware of them, he continues to sell the client because of his desire to sell as much as possible and to make a larger profit.
c. Has allowed the relationship between himself and the client to become a personal and possibly a social one.
d. Considers it beneath his dignity to ask a client for money.
e. Allows the client to soft soap him, flatter him, feed his ego—anything except to pay him.
f. Or is just too plain lazy or scared to go after his money in a strong and effective manner.

A substantial unpaid balance at the completion of a job not only endangers the designer's credit rating with trade sources, but gives rise to many other problems:

1. **Allowances and Adjustments**
When a client owes a designer a large balance, he may feel that he has the designer over a barrel so to speak. The writer has seen many situations in which the client, applying the threat of refusing to pay his balance, demands and secures unwarranted adjustments and allowances. (There should be no question that there are situations where a designer is responsible for adjustments but this is not our subject.) A favorite gambit used by clients relates to the fact that many jobs are installed on a piecemeal basis. In such cases, as furnishings are com-

pleted and delivered, there is a certain amount of wear and tear on the items delivered early in the job, so that these are not as new or fresh looking as the last items delivered. How many times has a client said to a designer, "This table shows liquor stains, or it's scratched," (after several months use) or "the fabric is discolored, etc., etc." and "I want it fixed before I 'settle with you'." Too many designers go along with this in their quest for a "harmonious relationship with a client" and because they are afraid to lose every dollar the client owes them.

2. **Return of Merchandise**
Even when designers follow the proper procedures—collecting deposits, signed confirmations, and so forth—some clients find, after the delivery of an item which they wanted, that it does not please them. If the client owes the designer a lot of money he is more likely to try to get away with a demand that it be returned: "I don't like it—I don't want it—Take it back." What is the designer to do in such a case? Actually the designer should stand on his two feet and refuse to do anything about it. Often, however, for the sake of "harmony," he will take it back and place it in his own inventory. Some of these inventory items can be resold, but some end up as furnishings in the designer's own home. Sometimes the designer can properly place these items on other jobs.

3. **Changes in a Client's Situation During the Progress of a Job**
With reference to monies due to a designer for orders placed and balances due for merchandise delivered, the designer must be aware of the complications that can result from:

A. The death of a client during the progress of a job. If letters of agreement are obtained at the inception of a job, there is a spelling out of responsibility. Generally the estate or surviving spouse would be responsible. If unpaid balances are not large, the settlement problems are, of course, less troublesome.

B. Divorce or separation. In today's world, divorce and separation are not unusual at all, but what if the contingency arises while the designer is in the middle of the job. If the designer has followed a sound procedure of:

1. Letter of agreement.
2. Signed confirmations.
3. 50% deposits.
4. Frequent billing and collection resulting in a minor accounts receivable balance—

Then his position is not too bad except in the cancellation of orders in progress. If the designer has, however, failed to provide coverage for himself, he may find that while his clients are battling for separation from each other, he will be fighting not to be separated from his money.

Conversely, a situation like the following can develop: A designer was doing a design installation for a bachelor client. Midway in the job, after orders had been placed and some items already delivered, the bachelor decided to get married. His wife-to-be did not want his bachelor apartment or the selected furnishings. The client then tried to walk away from the job by refusing to pay his bills and refusing to accept delivery of items previously ordered. The only solution available to the designer was to sell whatever finished items he could and to institute a lawsuit (based upon the letter of agreement and signed confirmations).

C. Changes in relationship between designer and client during progress of the job. It is the writers' opinion that as far as a designer's relationship with his clients are concerned, a clean separation should be maintained between the business and social phases of his life. Because an interior design installation for a residence is based upon personal understanding and because a designer is apt to work closely with a client, it is easy for social rapport to build up among all these "nice people." This can be extremely dangerous if the business relationship is allowed to soften and dissolve. To illustrate an actual situation:

Designer and client entered into a letter of agreement for a design job and at the inception the designer carried out the proper procedures of confirmation, deposit, and billing. As the job proceeded, the designer and client became quite friendly. Soon the client told the designer that confirmations and deposits and all such formality were unnecessary. The designer went along with this because now they were "friends."

When the job was completed and installed, the client owed a substantial balance to the designer. At that point disagreement arose between the two "friends." They ceased to be friends, and the designer found himself without a good substantial "paper" background of documentation to turn over to his attorney. As a result, he lost a substantial sum in the settlement. Whether the designer does or does not decide to become a friend of his client, he should never forget his primary obligations as a designer-businessman.

4. **Legal Action**
The final step in problems of this sort is turning the matter over to an attorney for legal action.

Legal actions are costly and unpleasant in most instances. However, if the designer has proceeded meticulously with the business procedures we have stated and restated, emphasized and re-emphasized—with the letter of agreement, signed confirmation, deposit, and maintenance of minimum possible accounts receivable balances—he will be able to give his attorney every possible bit of ammunition to resolve the case satisfactorily. The best possible rule to follow is to do everything possible within reason to resolve a conflict with a client, but if you must engage in legal action, first, be prepared, and second, don't be afraid to take the step.

Part 3 Non-Residential Work—Special Requirements

Chapter Sixteen

The Non-Residential Field as a Market for the Professional Interior Designer

The economic impact of the professional interior designer has made itself even more dramatically apparent in the non-residential or "contract" field than in the residential field. While the rising demand for professional interior designers in the residential field is an almost automatic reflection of population factors, growing wealth, and a cultural obsession with interiors as a status symbol and facet of the good life, in the non-residential field a rather more special phenomenon is evident—a remarkable change in the customs and attitudes of big institutions and business organizations. In many such, it was once the housekeeping staff who typically decided what furnishings were needed, and it was the wholesale dealer who supplied these furnishings.

Today, however, few people in top management are blind to the crucial importance of interior design as a factor in the success and efficiency of any business operation. They realize that the problem is not to procure furniture and other objects but to make certain that their expensive physical plant accomplishes its purpose—whether that purpose is to create an image and attract the public—as in a hotel, motel, restaurant, shop, or lobby; or to promote the efficiency and comfort of the working staff —as in an office; or many purposes combined.

Up-to-date executives realize that institutional and business environment has to work both physically and psychologically, both functionally and esthetically. The traffic patterns, furniture layouts, lighting, interior surfacings, window treatments, furniture, fabrics, colors, ornamentation, signs, symbols, graphics, and works of art are inextricably related factors in one integrated whole—one total though complex design. The professional person who understands how human beings relate to all these factors, who is trained to cope with them all separately and together, and who is qualified to produce that

one total design is the interior designer. This, too, is understood by the business community.

But non-residential work is big business involving big money. The interior designer has to adjust to many collaborators and many bosses, all of whom demand impeccable business conduct of him; on top of this he has to contend with competition.

Where the job is in a given edifice—perhaps an outdated building being remodeled or adapted to a new use—or a tenant space in an all-purpose building shell—the interior designer may well be in charge of the job, working alone as space planner and designer with or without such technical consultants as electrical engineers or air-conditioning experts. Where the job consists of a new edifice being built for the owner's operation—be it headquarters office, hotel, motel, school, or whatever—the interior designer most often collaborates with the building architect. Ideally, the interior designer joins the collaborative team at the outset, when the important decisions are made, when the plans are in discussion—rather than when nothing more remains to be decided except the colors and fabrics. The interior designer should even have a voice in *architectural* decisions, for the best way to insure a well-functioning building is to design it from the inside out; the interiors, after all, are the reason for the building. (There are, of course, *other* imperatives in architectural decisions; the size of the plot or the cost of land may dictate a tall building small in area despite the fact that a broad, low building might be less expensive to build and operate, pleasanter for its occupants, and more efficient for its purpose.)

In any case collaboration between architect and interior designer is commonplace today, so commonplace that many architectural firms are developing their own interior design staffs in order to control the design and to assure the simultaneous solution of interior and building design problems.

It is not only architectural firms, however, who find it advisable to employ captive interior design staffs. All kinds of big institutions and enterprises who must continually contend with the building and maintenance of physical plants are hiring staff designers—sometimes to do all the interiors for the company's buildings, and sometimes only to coordinate the work and develop programs to be carried through by independent interior designers hired for specific jobs. This is true of many hotel/motel, restaurant, and store chains as well as many branches of government. The trend to maintaining corporate staff designers reflects the average executive's new sophistication and knowledgeability on the competitive importance of flair, style, and elegance in a visually expressed image.

The enormous demand for talent triggered by this trend is tempting many interior design firms with a reputation for creative originality to explore the non-residential field. Most of them are finding it very lucrative indeed—in spite of the fact that their organizations are relatively small, and in spite of the fact that they have not acquired expertise in delivering mass volume jobs that call for mass purchasing.

Essentially, Part Three of this book—consisting of five chapters on the special problems of working in the non-residential field—is addressed to the kind of firm just defined, the small or medium-sized firm of independent interior designers who want to proceed smoothly and safely into non-residential work. This does not mean that the practices recommended here are invalid for interior design departments within architectural firms or corporations, but that some of the bookkeeping procedures do not apply, since the architectural and business offices have control procedures and accounting systems of their own.

In passing we might mention that there are other kinds of firms which are finding it profitable to maintain captive departments of professionally qualified interior designers. Among these are many large retail establishments—both general department stores and furniture and home furnishings stores. Such stores may have only a residential interior design department or both a residential and non-residential design department. Another type of establishment in which large staffs of A.I.D. and N.S.I.D. members can be found are wholesale regional dealerships, sometimes specializing in office furniture and sometimes covering every sector of work. It goes without saying that such stores and wholesale dealerships also have their own highly organized business procedures and policies. They have discovered that the only way to assure business is to offer not merely merchandise but a complete design service package.

The derivation of the term *contract field* or *contract design* commonly used as a synonym for *non-residential* is hard to trace, but one can assume that it implies the contracting (and subcontracting) or mass purchases of goods and services. It must be admitted that all of these terms are slightly inaccurate since contracting occurs often in residential work, and the "non-residential" field covers such residential installations as lobbies, hotels, and dormitories, while many small or executive office jobs are handled like residential jobs as far as business procedures are concerned. The key question in defining residential work is whether or not the work is for an *individual* client's *personal* occupancy.

Chapter Seventeen

Initial Client Contact in Non-Residential Work

The initial stage of negotiations—when the designer and potential client make contact, sound each other out on the possibility of a project, and perhaps come to terms—is even more crucial in the non-residential than in the residential field (where the subject was covered in Chapter 6). The job can be much larger, the client's criteria more impersonal, and the situation more competitive. Because the client is a person or group in top management, and the job entails a large investment for productive or functional purposes, the designer's proposals must be rationalized clearly and minutely. The designer's whole approach must be far more positive and elaborately prepared. Selling is a more important function, and the communications between client and designer are often extremely formalized and detailed, to assure that the designer gets a complete picture of the client's program and that the client gets a complete picture of the designer's proposed solution for that program. The determination of fees and arrangements for the awarding of the job are also time-consuming and meticulous.

To attract a steady flow of new clients, many of the larger interior design firms specializing in non-residential work have over the years developed systematic selling and publicity programs. Some of them even advertise in business papers and periodicals, or in the business and real estate sections of newspapers. Advertising is still a moot question in the interior design field, largely because the architectural establishment frowns on advertising as "unprofessional", and straightforward advertising is rare, though the names and faces of many residential and non-residential interior designers appear in advertisements of products in space paid for by the manufacturers. Nevertheless there are a number of advertisements placed by non-residential firms in business papers which are so dignified and to the point that accusations of unprofessional behavior would be irrelevant. In any case, a pub-

licity program is part of any large non-residential firm's operations. Sometimes it is attended to by the principal, as one of his many duties; sometimes it is assigned to a full-time employee with professional qualifications in journalism and public relations; and sometimes the firm retains an outside public relations representative. The relative advantages and disadvantages of each system is beyond the scope of this work, but it is certain that some part of the budget of the big firm in the non-residential field is devoted to promotion.

In the big firms, the job of selling also tends to be assigned to a specific principal. Thus one member of the firm devotes the greater part of his time not to creative design but to communicating with potential clients, conferring with them to set down the facts concerning the jobs they have pending, and organizing and presenting proposals (for which the creative work will probably be done by other members of the staff). The fact that big firms have a staff allowing this kind of specialization is one of the most important advantages of bigness. In smaller firms the problem of doing both selling and creative work adequately is a never-ending dilemma. All too often the head of the firm finds, after completing a superbly performed job, that he is without work to cover his payroll and overhead for the next period because he did not take time out to bring in new jobs. (Architectural firms are subject to the same problem.)

Conversely, many talented interior designers bewail the fact that once they achieve fame and fortune, the pressure of business keeps them out of the office on a perennial selling tour instead of at the drawing board. The solution which all firms aim for is a happy balance between good creative and good selling staff. The selling staff, after all, have to be professionally competent in design, since they must dig out the essence of the client's program and tastes, and must succeed in communicating the creative ideas as well as the planning rationale of the proposed solutions to their own colleagues.

A growing reputation makes the chore of lining up new work easier with the passing years. But it is important to bear in mind that this reputation has to encompass not only esthetic creativity but procedural know-how. In reviewing a firm's record, business people give weight not only to the excitement and elegance of their work but to such matters as to whether the installations were successful for the clients, whether the materials lasted, whether the jobs were completed on time and for the estimated budgets.

Notwithstanding these formidable criteria, many of the smaller firms are gaining ground in the field and competing successfully against the giants with a combination of free-wheeling creativity, careful business analysis of the clients' programs, and rigid discipline in their own business procedures. For the smaller firms are not without advantages of their own. They are apt to be more flexible, to offer more freedom and opportunity to the creative staff, and to carry less deadwood on the payroll.

To compete successfully in the non-residential field, the interior designer must consider in a new light the following elements and processes:

1. The initial approach to the client
2. Understanding the job
3. The presentation
4. The determination of a fee basis
5. The letter of agreement
6. The responsibility for purchases
7. Installation dates.

1. **The Initial Approach to the Client.**
In non-residential work, the image projected by the firm is of signal importance in selling its services. The potential client must have no doubt that he will be working with a responsible organization. Fame and recommendations may lead corporate executives to the design firm, but almost never spur them to make a definite offer unless the firm presents a soundly conceived design solution and indicates that its business practices are sound as well. Unless a corporation has had such exceptionally successful results with one design firm that it decides to give all its work to that firm, it normally approaches two or more design firms on the possibility of doing the job; when the designer is contacted by a new client he can take it for granted that his proposals and his organization are being compared with those of a competitor. His own offices will be inspected as an example of his work and as an indication of his operational solidity. The personality of the staff member who makes the presentation is important. So are the design proposals, of course—not only the esthetic solution for the job but the planning analysis and the cost breakdown.

Whether the first interview is in the client's headquarters or the designer's, the designer or his representative should have background material on his work—especially in projects similar to the client's, if possible—unless of course the designer is exceptionally famous and has just made the front pages with some spectacular project. Reprints of published work, brochures, photographs, and slides should be assembled for a presentation that will answer the client's questions about the firm's capabilities and experience.

During this meeting the designer must also

elicit necessary information. It goes without saying that if he has done his homework he will have boned up on the history of the client's organization and the character and tastes of the executives with whom he will be dealing. But he must also find out enough about the prospective job to enable him rationally to answer two crucial questions:

1. Is the job within his (or his firm's) capabilities, or is it too big, too complicated, or too unfamiliar? Will he be biting off more than he can chew?
2. Has he grasped the client's wishes sufficiently to enable him to work out a suggested solution within the client's concepts, tastes, and budget?

2. **Understanding the Job.**
The initial meeting should produce no other result than the exchange of necessary information acquainting the client and the design firm with each other and the design firm with the general nature of the proposed job. The designer should definitely not attempt to answer any specific questions about how he might solve the design problem, what the job might cost, how much he would charge, or how he might arrive at a fee.

The cardinal rule to follow at this point in the negotiations is that before any solution—or even any approach to a solution can be found, the designer must have a *thorough understanding of the scope and requirements of the job*. Without a complete grasp of the situation, neither concept nor costs, nor fees can be arrived at. If, in his eagerness, the designer rushes into a guesstimate, he runs a strong risk of being dangerously wrong on every factor. The businessman client will respect the designer who firmly

answers that he cannot quote on the job until he has had the opportunity to make a thorough study of the requirements and a meticulous estimate of the necessary time. The designer must take this position and then proceed to gather and analyze the following information:

A. *Pertaining to the nature of the job*
Have you come away from the initial conference with complete information as to what the client wants with regard to:

1. the design concept?
2. the nature, size, and location of all the areas included?
3. the budget?
4. purchasing—whether to be done by the design firm or the client?
5. relationships with architects or contractors?
6. installation timing or deadline?

B. *Pertaining to the nature of the service expected of the designer*
Will it be to do the—
1. design concept only?
2. design concept and supplying of materials and services?
3. space planning?
4. specifying architectural or structural alterations?
    —working with architects?
    —working with contractors?
5. furnishing requirements?
    —purchasing from regular trade sources?
    —or preparing specifications for special construction?
6. amount of estimated required time at the drafting board?
7. shopping time and market trips?
8. preparation of purchase specifications?

99

9. supervision of sources?
10. supervision of work at the job site?
11. storage requirements?
12. supervision of installation?

C. *Pertaining to the client's budget*

What funds are available for the job? This is one of the most essential facts for the designer to obtain at the first meeting. The designer's proposals must relate to this sum. If he does not have at least a realistic approximate figure, his design concept is just a stab in the dark. The cleverest and most original solution based upon too high or too low a figure can appear so ludicrous as to assure that the designer will lose the job. Experience can in certain situations provide a general yardstick. The designer may know, for example, that a modest motel room may cost between $800 and $1,100 to furnish; but the possible differential in the cost of a ballroom is too broad even for generalized guesswork.

In spite of this, many clients who have not taken the trouble to analyze their own requirements thoroughly will impose upon designers bidding for a job by asking that they propose both what appears to them to be a reasonable budget and a design concept within that budget. Unaware of many factors in the client's situation which the client has not divulged, the designer has an excellent chance of aiming wide of the mark and losing the job even if he works very hard at developing proposals, as the following example illustrates: Two design firms were asked to develop a concept and a budget for a showroom. No budget was specified, not even a vague span. Without clues of any kind, the first firm took an elegant approach, while the second opted for simplicity and functionalism. The difference in cost between the two

was substantial, and the client, lacking the amount of money needed to realize the first design, gave the job to the second firm. Once the decision was made, however, he asked the second firm to develop the job in the elegant style proposed by the first firm—but lowering costs by cutting corners in the amount of detailing and the quality of materials. It is unnecessary to emphasize that the first firm was victimized by this unbusinesslike and unethical procedure, and that it is not wise to compete on this kind of blind budget basis.

Some potential clients will indicate in good faith that their primary consideration is the design concept rather than costs, and that the budget can be worked out with management once the design concept is accepted. This may provide a base solid enough for the building of a concept provided that the general budget area at least is known and that the client makes his wants very clear. But in general the potential client in the non-residential field will have a fair idea of the capital commitment he is facing before he undertakes any major change in his plant.

D. *Other factors to be considered*
1. Credit standing of potential clients
   a. Obtain reports from credit agency
   b. Obtain information from bank

2. Distance from the designer's office
   a. Travel and subsistence costs of staff

3. Availability of local trade sources and labor

4. Designated working representatives of the client
   a. In working on a country club, do you answer to the manager, a committee, the

president, or the entire membership?

The designer who approaches a new non-residential client with concern for all of the aforementioned factors will be armed with sufficient information to prepare a workmanlike presentation—one based upon the client's actual design requirements, upon his financial framework, upon the actual capabilities of the designer's organization, and upon the required compatibility between designer and client.

3. **The Presentation.**
In the non-residential field, the formal presentation has become standard business procedure. The designer presents the design concept, based upon the client's program and possibly upon the designer's further research into the conditions of the job. His illustrations may include renderings or sketches or plans or models or any combination of these and other visual media including samples, and they will be accompanied by facts and figures analyzing the planning approach to the job, and the estimated budget, the method of arriving at a fee, and the fee itself. The presentation is made to management at a conference-lecture, usually including a question-and-answer period, and then left with management for their review. Some presentations are virtually competitive bids by firms which are being considered for the job, while other presentations are made by firms already chosen to do the job, with only the final design concept to be discussed by management and possibly revised at their request.

Since the development of a presentation is time-consuming and costly, the designer must make two initial decisions regarding:

A. payment for the presentation, and

B. the depth of pictorial and statistical information to be compiled for it.

A. *Should the interior designer expect to be paid for making a presentation?*
Or should he cover the cost himself, either including it among his development or selling expenses for winning the job (if he does win it) or with the firm's promotional budget? Exactly the same dilemma faces architectural firms. Practically and pragmatically speaking, there is no hard and fast rule. The factors involved in the firm's decision are related to a similar dilemma which arises in estimating the costs of a job in order to bid for it—and in fact it may involve one and the same operation, since a presentation includes both a proposed design solution and and an estimate of what it will cost to realize that design solution (although it is possible to make a design concept presentation without fully estimating the costs, where the client specifies a "price-no-object-job," which is hardly typical). The problem is discussed again in the following chapter, devoted to fees and compensations, in the section on speculative bidding.

Firms which answer the question in the negative, who are, that is, prepared to cover the costs of preparing presentations out of their own operating or promotional budgets, rationalize the decision on the ground that without job promotion there are no jobs, no profits, no anything.

Firms which answer the question with a resounding *yes!*—firms which refuse to make a presentation (or to prepare a bid for a job or a cost estimate for a job related to a design concept for that job) unless the potential client first agrees to cover their costs, are those who

101

are so sought after that they have more potential clients than they can serve.

But there is more to be considered than whether the firm is hungry for work or in the happy position of being able to pick and choose its jobs. It is also extremely important to differentiate between situations where the client will use the presentation as the basis for his choice of a firm to do the job, asking two or more firms to make presentations on a competitive basis, *or* where the client has chosen the design firm for his job before a fully developed design concept has been agreed upon.

The very life of the new young firm and the hungry firm may depend on its getting the job. The designer may feel that he has no choice but to make a pitch, putting every ounce of energy and imagination into his effort to dazzle the potential client. If he believes in himself, his enthusiasm is certainly an asset, and many firms have won their first foothold in the field by just this kind of all-out effort in a speculative presentation.

The serious catch—there is always a catch in a speculative procedure—is, of course, that the potential client may merely be out to do some brain picking, having already decided on an inexpensive firm to carry the work through once the client has skimmed the cream off a few presentations. Or there may be other reasons why the design firm hasn't a chance of winning the job even though several firms have been invited to make competitive presentations or bids. Not too rarely, the executives of a corporation may make up their minds about a design firm but go through the motions of considering other competitors because the regulations or policies of the organization demand this, in which case the

unsuccessful competitors are merely being used for the purpose of an attractive report to the stockholders.

It is, therefore, important, before deciding to prepare a speculative presentation or speculative bid, to find out as much as possible about the potential client's record in its dealings with interior designers, architects, contractors, and builders. There are good and bad, honest and dishonest, difficult and easy clients, and the extreme cases often acquire widespread reputations. The worst should be avoided no matter how hungry the designer may be.

For in the end all costs have to be covered in one way or another, and whether or not the client pays for a presentation on a job he turned down from a designer he did not hire, the designer has to cover the cost somehow. His only source of income are clients, and if he does not recover the cost of an unsuccessful presentation from the client he doesn't get, he must recover it from the clients he has.

The decisions involved here are not entirely in the realm of accounting, but in the much more fluid area of selling strategy and the sparring of personalities. One classic strategem of the hungry firm or unemployed individual is to put up a good front and play hard-to-get, and there is, of course, no rule of thumb to foresee when it will and will not work. The bargaining position of both parties is affected by the imponderables of the negotiators' intelligence, character, and persistence.

Very different is the situation where the potential client is no longer in fact potential but already committed to a particular designer. In such a case the purpose of the presentation is not to determine who will get the job but to enable the client—whether he is an individual or a managerial board—to review the designer's proposals and possibly suggest certain alterations. Here the question of payment for the presentation merely involves bookkeeping procedures, since, of course, the time expense will be covered in the designer's fee in one way or another. In extremely big jobs with complex requirements, the designer may make two or more presentations before client management will give final approval.

The dilemma of competitive presentations and competitive bidding can be observed very often in formal competitions, particularly architectural competitions. Architectural competitions, of course, are a time-honored procedure for the awarding of extremely important commissions, particularly where the government or an institution is the client.

Yet even there the commission is considered a plum from every point of view; it is a known fact that when work is plentiful, the most important architectural firms will refuse to enter competitions since they are hard put to complete the work they are committed to, let alone diverting expensive staff to a project which they have only one chance in, let's say, ten, of winning. Therefore, speculative architectural competitions are used today only in situations where the sponsor wants specifically to discover an unknown talent, or a young designer. Such competitions tend to be relatively unimportant because even if the discovered talent is very real, such a designer is not likely to have the practical experience to enable him to estimate costs and carry through the job, so that the sponsor stands to bear further expenses in the project's specifying and structural stages.

Where sponsors want top-ranking architectural firms to compete, therefore, they conduct an *invited* competition, in which each competitor is paid a nice round fee—covering costs, overhead, and profits—simply to compete. Or the sponsor can organize a two-stage competition, in which the first stage calls only for a relatively undetailed plan and concept, and the second for the full development.

Since relatively less time and staff need be invested in the first stage, it does not cost too much to compete, so that if the sponsor chooses to invite many competitors, his costs are not astronomical. Or if the sponsor chooses not to pay entrants for their work on the first stage of the competition, good firms may not be discouraged from entering if, at least, the project is challenging. In such a case the big fees arise only in the competition's second stage, for which finalists are chosen by the competition jury.

Such systems are excellent ways of getting top-ranking firms to compete, or of getting both talented unknowns as well as top-ranking firms into the picture. And these systems have obvious parallels in the procedures of big corporations or institutions looking for interior designers (or architects, or other related professionals) to take on their work.

The negotiations carried on by interior design firms may be complicated by the fact that negotiations with a building architect may be going on at the same time. If the architect who wins the building commission has his own interior design department, he will, of course, try to get the contract for the interiors as well. In the writer's opinion, he ought to, since the building and interior concept should be inseparable. This does not apply, however, if the building architect is designing an anonymous shell or merely doing structural alterations or remodeling in a building. In any case interior design departments in architectural firms don't necessarily win the commissions for the interiors of their firms' jobs, and more and more such departments are taking on interiors for buildings being designed by other architectural firms, or interiors in situations where an architect may be incidental or totally absent—so that the only parties to the negotiations are the interior designer (or his representative) and the client (or corporate building commission).

It is a pity that client-designer negotiations are often comparable to a sparring or fencing match—warlike games—but few design firms are so loaded with work that they can send a client packing when they suspect he is capable of exploiting them. The design firms can protect themselves by making dignified professional demeanor and effectively projected businesslike procedures a matter of routine. Clients, like everyone else, need to be educated as to the meaning and worth of professional service. The first time a client becomes a client may set a pattern for his future attitudes to any and all design firms he deals with. The design firm needs to sell its services, needs to get the job, but also needs to educate the client. Where it becomes clear that a client is intractable or dishonest, then it is better not to start, since it is possible to win clients and go broke.

B. *How deep a presentation should the design firm prepare?*

A design firm's presentation may range from a brief conference in which a few pencil sketches and freehand floor plans, accompanied by a page or two of typed material explaining the analysis of the program and a rough approximation of cost estimates, to a complete economic and operational analysis of the client's operations, present and future, a projection of future space and traffic needs as well as those specified by the client for present needs, elaborate studies of the physical and psychological requirements of the staff which will occupy the client's premises, and a thoroughly developed space plan, esthetic system, and designs for custom furniture and equipment as well as stock furniture and equipment. The visual material may include presentation boards, models, full-size mock-ups, color renderings, color, fabric, and other material samples, photographs, slides, floor plans, and full-scale booklets or other bound typed or printed material. The same common-sense strictures apply to the decisions about how deeply to proceed as about whether to expect payment. The strategy and warnings cited in Chapter 6 on "Initial Client Contacts in the Residential Field" apply in the non-residential field, only more so. Preparing elaborate presentations or even divulging brilliantly original ideas is a risky undertaking if the client is neither committed to the designer nor paying him to prepare the presentation. If the client is formally committed or paying the designer to make a presentation (or bid for the job), the situation is, of course, entirely different.

The answer to both of our key questions about presentations lies in the character of the client, his experience as a client, and his attitude towards professional service.

4. **Determining the Fee or Compensation Base.**
It is not enough to prepare a design concept as a base for a discussion with potential clients. It is equally essential to think through the question of the fee or compensation base. Every cli-

ent wants to know what he is going to pay for a proposed service, and businessmen will not accept indefinite proposals. The designer must take a stand as to what fee basis is right for the job and for his organization. For the determination of the fee base is a complicated procedure in which the decisive factors are a full understanding of the nature of the full scope of services to be performed, and it is the subject of the next chapter. The point to be made here is simply that this analytical procedure must be thoroughly performed by the designer, so that when he negotiates with the client about the design solution he knows exactly how the work involved is to be charged for. Once having arrived at a full understanding of this, he should be able to explain it to the client. And he had better be prepared to stick to his guns if the client tries to cut him down.

5. The Letter of Agreement.

It is not necessary to have a letter of agreement completed and ready for signature at the presentation meeting. However, since it is usual and normal for financial and job conditions to be discussed to some extent at the first few meetings, the designer should by that time be fully cognizant of the conditions of the job and be able to bring the various problems into focus. Thus, when the client acknowledges the selection of the designer and the time comes to prepare the letter of agreement, all of its component parts will have been blocked out, at least roughly, in previous discussions, so that the designer will be ready to prepare the letter and the client will find no surprises in it. The subject is discussed in Chapter 19.

6. Responsibility for Purchases.

In the residential field it is normal procedure for the designer not only to place the orders for the purchases of goods and services, but to assume the financial liability of paying the suppliers. In the non-residential field, however, the extent of such purchases is so enormous that a designer had better think hard before assuming the financial liabilities involved. In an average-sized hotel job, for example, the designer may specify about a million dollars in purchases. Early in the meetings with new non-residential clients, the designer should find out whether the clients' firm has a purchasing department of its own. If so, the standard procedure is for the designer to provide the client with purchase specifications so that the orders are placed directly by the client. With larger clients, it is an ideal situation to have them follow the procedure of ordering materials and services and assuming the liabilities which arise. This procedure is ideal. The office procedure for the designer is covered in Chapter 26 under Exhibit B (purchase requisitions). In the case of a client whose organization is too small to have a purchasing department, and there is no one in the company accustomed to the tasks involved, so that the client prefers to have the designer's firm place the orders, it is essential that the designer first check the client's credit rating. If it is good, and the purchases involved are not astronomical, then the designer may probably proceed safely provided that 1) he demands substantial deposits against the placing of orders, and 2) follows meticulously the proper procedures for the routing of orders in the section on *purchase requisition* in Chapter 13.

7. Installation Dates.

The installation date for a non-residential job is a serious commitment. From the first meeting the designer should begin to analyze the time requirements so that he can estimate a reasonable time program, and if the client has a deadline in mind, the designer can express a valid opinion about it. All business concerns commit themselves to a planned schedule of activities, and base their operations and their contracts for future business on such schedules. Simultaneously they commit themselves to specified capital outlays. They cannot allow either their business programs or their capital to be jeopardized by the failure of a design firm to meet its dates.

If the date proposed by the client is unrealistic, the designer should make the fact—and the reasons—clear to the client, and should refuse to take the job unless the deadline is corrected. The interior designer should also be extremely wary of signing an agreement containing a penalty clause for failing to meet specified installation dates. For the designer can never completely control the flow of products and services from the innumerable sources involved. The best he can do with respect to this factor, is to choose his sources carefully, selecting those that have given him prompt delivery in the past, and to base his installation schedule on such experiences. The designer should also be aware of delays that may be caused by the client's own inefficiency in approving design details or purchase orders. If the letter of agreement or penalty clause threaten the designer in case of late installation, the designer in turn should see to it that the client's responsibilties for prompt action in his part of the required procedures are also clearly spelled out. And all reasonable disclaimers of responsibility in case of disasters or failures of contractors or sources beyond the designer's control should be included.

Chapter Eighteen

Non-Residential—
Fees and Compensations

In the non-residential field the scope and variety of jobs that designers may be called upon to do and the services they may render are so unlimited that standard rules and charts for setting fees are useless. The only rational approach to the selection of a proper fee or compensation base for any job—but above all for any non-residential job—is through a thorough analysis of that job.

Emphasis was placed on this importance of understanding the nature of each specific job in the previous chapter, devoted to the initial contact with the client. To facilitate this analysis we outlined several check lists of information which the designer should gather. The scope of services and the client's budget are the two focal elements in the designer's study to determine which of the available fee bases (or combinations thereof) will be most remunerative and logical for the work involved. The choice of a fee base can be substantially affected by the previous experiences of a design firm. The accumulation and analysis of the cost records of completed jobs can be of invaluable help if the designer succeeds in relating factors and conditions in a new job to similar factors in a completed job where the financial returns are known.

The first step, then, is to estimate, on the basis of information gathered in the initial meeting or meetings with the client, how much time is likely to be needed to complete the various phases of the work. In addition, the designer should know whether purchasing will be included in the scope of the work, and whether it can be used as a basis for determining compensation.

As an illustration let us take a potential job involving a new hotel under construction. A meeting with the management revealed that the designer's function was to consist of the following:

1. To design, lay out, and select furnishings for
   400 typical bedrooms—with two-color schemes
   20 typical parlors—with one-color scheme
   4 executive suites—with one-color scheme
   8 public corridors
2. To prepare two complete color scheme books of typical layouts
3. To prepare two complete furniture and furnishings books
4. To prepare two typical layout books
5. To prepare furniture layout plans
6. To select and specify types of furniture, fabrics, paint colors, floor coverings, lighting fixtures, lamps, and accessories.
7. To consult and/or select color and materials for toilet areas
8. To make a final inspection of the installation

The analysis indicated that the designer would *not* be responsible for the following: He was—

1. Not to place orders for the purchases, but merely specify the type and management would procure on its own
2. Not to be responsible for the assembling of the items for installation
3. Not to be responsible for actual installation

As a result of the analysis, the design firm determined that:

A. Since it was not doing the purchasing, a mark-up on purchases could not be the compensation base.
B. Since the client was doing both the installation and purchasing, the *Complete Installation Price* method could not be used either.
C. The only compensation methods left as a result of the foregoing analysis of the job were either the flat fee or the fee based on time charges. Further conferences with the client eliminated

the time-charge base, and, therefore, a flat fee had to be computed. It was evolved in the following way:

Each area of phase of the work was analyzed to indicate which employee would be assigned to it and how many hours would be budgeted for it. A final compilation was then set up in the following schedule:

Principal	50 hours @ $50.	$ 2,500.
Job Captain	100 hours @ $25.	$ 2,500.
Draftsmen	120 hours @ $21.	$ 2,520.
Designer	150 hours @ $21.	$ 3,150.
Shopper	75 hours @ $15.	$ 1,125.
Clerical Assistant	100 hours @ $10.	$ 1,000.
Total	595 hours	$12,795.

The design firm checked its records of two similar jobs it had recently completed and found that they averaged approximately 500 hours, with fees about $15,000 each. Using all of this information, the firm quoted a fee of $15,000 for the job, which was accepted by the client. The *time work-up* was based upon employee productivity costs discussed in Chapter 23.

The job might at first seem enormous, and difficult to relate to other jobs, but upon analysis all that it turned out to consist of was:

A. Five layouts (two for the bedrooms, one for the parlors, one for the executive suites and one for the public corridors).
B. Selection of the furnishings.
C. Setting forth the specifications and instructions in a form that would enable the client to proceed with ordering and installation.

The fee was realistic in terms of the requirements of the job. The analysis made by the design firm on the basis of its own past experiences proved sound, as is indicated by the fact that they won the job and on its conclusion found that they earned a profit on it.

The determination of a basis for computing compensation for non-residential work may be further complicated by the range of the firm's activities. The factors to be considered vary, depending upon whether the firm is:

1. Engaged in non-residential work exclusively
2. Engaged in both non-residential and residential work
3. Engaged primarily in residential work, only occasionally becoming involved in a non-residential job.

1. The firm engaged solely in non-residential work is usually large enough to afford a proper cost accounting system and technical business counsel to guide it properly in preparing the data needed for the selection of a fee basis and computation of fees. In organizations of this type, the productive hours of the creative staff—designers, draftsmen, job captains, shoppers, and supervisors—are the key source producing the income to cover all general and administrative overhead.

Positive information on operating expenses must be in hand if these expenses are to be related to the cost of the productive hours to be billed. Normally these productive hours are billed at three times the payroll cost; this is the amount needed to cover operating expenses and allow a reasonable profit as well.

2. The firm engaged in both residential and non-

residential work requires the same basic information as the firm engaged in non-residential work for arriving at a fee basis for the non-residential work. Therefore, the firm's accounting system should provide for separate records for the residential and non-residential work in order to build up sets of historical records reflecting the scope of the non-residential jobs, their billing price, costs, time expenditures, and resulting profits. These records are an essential asset to the firm as a reference for the review of compensation bases in preparing to quote fees for potential jobs.

3. Many one-man design firms work primarily in the residential field, finding themselves involved in non-residential work only at rare intervals. For them the prospect of quoting a fee for non-residential work poses a monumental task, since they have very little experience to use as a reference. Nevertheless they can use the same concepts which apply to larger firms, perhaps with some modifications.

Regardless of the size of the design firm, the concepts and principles involved in the evaluation of the fee or compensation base are the same, namely:

A. An understanding of the nature of the job

B. A sound analysis of the scope of the job

C. A knowledge of the client's budget requirements

D. A clarification of other pertinent factors peculiar to that particular job to be gained in meetings with the client

E. A complete understanding of employee productivity costs and time valuation for billing purposes.

Selecting the Fee or Compensation Base

After the potential job has been carefully analyzed and a time study of its various phases has been completed, a schedule will be developed along the following format:

Principal	25 hours @ $35.	$ 875.
Job Captain	50 hours @ $25.	$1,250.
Draftsmen	100 hours @ $21.	$2,100.
Shopping time	50 hours @ $15.	$ 750.
Supervision	40 hours @ $25.	$1,000.
Total		$5,975.

In this schedule, as usual, all time is charged at three times its actual payroll cost.

This indicates that the quotable fee or selected compensation base must bring in a minimum of $6,000. After giving consideration to all of the factors in the assignment, the designer can select from the following a fee base which will cover most situations:

1. Flat-fee basis
2. Percentage of cost of purchases made on behalf of the client
3. Fee for design work plus percentage of purchases
4. Time basis
5. Retail basis
6. Complete installation basis

1. *Flat-fee basis*

In the flat-fee basis the design firm requests a specific sum of money to cover the entire compensation exclusive of reimbursement for specific expenses. It can be considered a proper fee basis in the following cases:

a. When the job consists of design in all its

109

phases—planning, esthetic concept, detailing, selection of furnishings—but *not* purchasing on behalf of the client.

b. When the preliminary analysis of the job indicates that the purchasing of materials and supplies is to be for relatively small quantities in comparison to the time to be expended in designing, planning, detailing, supervising, installing, and any other functions apart from purchasing.

c. When working with a client who expects to relate his fee to the value of design services rendered and not to the size of the budget, so that if the large budget is used for multiple quantity purchases that involve relatively little design, the client will not agree to relate the size of the fee to the dollar volume of purchases.

d. When the time needed for the job can be estimated with reasonable certainty and the job requirements are definite and controllable. Assignments nebulous as to time requirements— for example to "do a special survey and make recommendations"—are risky in connection with the flat-fee basis.

2. *Percentage of the cost of purchases*
In this method the designer's compensation is computed as a percentage mark-up on the cost of all furnishings and services he purchases or specifies for a client. It is used to a great extent, and used effectively.

It can be used as the *exclusive* compensation base only when the *purchasing budgets are comparatively large* in relation to the amount of time to be expended on design, supervision, installation, and other professional services. The preliminary analysis of the job will indi-

cate whether the markup on cost will produce more or less compensation than the charging of a flat fee based on a preliminary estimate of time required.

Example:
Assume that the analysis projects the following factors:

A. Merchandise and services to be purchased at cost total $50,000.

B. The cost of estimated time required (at a billing price of 3X the payroll cost of staff) comes to $6,000.

Then, if the percentage mark-up is—
10%—the compensation will be $ 5,000.
15%—the compensation will be $ 7,500.
20%—the compensation will be $10,000.

This computation indicates clearly that the firm can take on this job on a mark-up basis of 15% to 20%, since the amount it will have to spend to cover overhead and labor (and this applies also to the one-man firm, so that the word *designer* can be substituted for *firm* in this paragraph) will come to less than the compensation for the job, leaving a profit. If the firm cannot get better than 10%, however, it will not cover its overhead, so that it must come up with some other compensation basis that will produce the required income (or the job should be turned down).

If, however, the merchandise and services to be purchased at cost amount to only $20,000 and the same amount of time is required, then the percentage mark-up cannot be used as a proper base for compensation. It is quite simple to determine the anticipated profit on a cost-plus project, and all that is then necessary is to interpret this profit in terms of the necessary expenditures of energy, money, and time to determine its relevancy.

3. *Fee for design service plus a mark-up on cost*
One excellent method of arriving at a justifiable compensation base is to combine a flat fee for the design service entailed in the job with a percentage mark-up on purchases. The method is ideal where the job entails both a sizable factor of time expended on design concept and development, as well as a heavy purchasing schedule. For design and board time, a design fee can be computed (either as a flat fee on estimated time requirements or on an hourly basis). And as payment for the firm's service in shopping, writing orders, writing specifications, supervising, and installing, a percentage mark-up on all purchases can be used. The percentage mark-up under these conditions can range between 5% and 10%, depending upon the size of the purchasing budget.

This method overcomes the reluctance of many clients to pay a fee based upon a high percentile mark-up and reflects the two different phases of the job—designing and purchasing—fairly in the income earned for these two phases. Again, the conditions stipulated by the client and the analysis of the job by the designer will indicate the potential effectiveness of this method.

4. *Time basis*
Under this method the designer and the client agree to base compensation upon the actual time expended by the designer and his staff on the job, according to predetermined hourly charge rates. The hourly charges can be stated for each individual member of the staff, or can be stated as a flat hourly average. It is essential that proper time records be maintained, indicating the employee, the nature of his work, the date, the time, and the hourly rate (as detailed in Chapter 23). Billings are rendered to clients with a full breakdown of the time charges.

This method results in an excellent compensation base for any design office, but meets with client resistance for many reasons, particularly the absence of any kind of ceiling over the final cost, and client reluctance to accept the credibility of time records. As far as the problem of the cost ceiling is concerned, it can be dealt with by agreeing to a predetermined limit on the fee—for it is possible to estimate a reasonable maximum time requirement with a *careful* analysis of the job. Such a limit protects the client against runaway time charges and overcomes the objections of many clients.

This method merits consideration for unusual jobs where the scope of services required of the design firm do not fall into the usual pattern. Consultation service is probably the best example. It is virtually impossible to estimate the amount of time that will be spent if the primary design service will be to consult with architects or project managers or the client's own design staff. (Consultation service should not, for that very reason, be undertaken with the *predetermined* time limit discussed in the previous paragraph.)

An excellent example of the application of the time-charge basis was a job to design and produce a floor of executive offices for a large corporation, developing each specific executive suite and such special areas as the executive reception, dining, and board rooms in accordance with the tastes and wishes of each individual executive or groups of executives who were to use the spaces involved, and also to satisfy the demands of an executive committee. Since design-concept time, market-research time, and shopping time could not be predetermined, it was agreed that the assignment could be taken only on the basis of compensation for actual time expended.

Of course, the question of the client's trust in the design firm is the perennial nagging drawback in such situations. To avoid being challenged on the veracity of his time records and on the need for using as much time as he did for whatever he did, a designer needs to conduct himself with unassailable authority and keep records of unassailable accuracy.

5. *Retail basis*
The definition of the *retail basis* of establishing fees is the same in the non-residential field as in the residential field (Chapter 9). It is the billing for furnishings and services at the equivalent of a full retail price. A design firm should definitely consider the application of the retail basis in the non-residential field in the following cases:

a. For small budget non-residential jobs involving expenditures of less than $10,000; such budgets do not generate enough profits to pay for the time and talent required on any fee basis except the retail basis.

b. For executive offices, which are similar to residential jobs in the way the designer works with the client, and in the absence of multiple orders for furnishings. Such jobs are non-residential in that the bills are paid by a corporation, but in working arrangements and profit factors they are like residential jobs, and like residential jobs lend themselves well to the retail basis.

6. *Complete installation basis*
The complete installation basis is the setting of one total fee for the complete range of services from the development of the concepts, layouts, specifications, through the purchase of all equipment to the final supervision of the installation. The preparation of this fee is similar to the process of bidding on a contract award.

If the design firm is bidding against competition for the job, and the potential client does not reveal the size of the proposed budget, the firm is risking the time required to develop the concept and prepare the estimate on a bid basis, simply hoping that his concept and cost proposals will win out over all other bids. This type of bidding should be avoided by designers without ample experience in the kind of job involved. Not only is the investment in time and work too great to risk in a speculative situation, but there is also the danger that in his eagerness to win the job the designer will make a bid so hopefully and unrealistically low that if it is accepted it will doom him to a financial loss.

But there are situations when the firm may be justified in undertaking the time-and-money consumming series of tasks involved in the preparation of a total estimate for a *turn-key job,* as jobs done on this basis are called. If the client divulges the budget figure, clearly specifies the preferences and ideas which will guide his final selection . . . and if the client's reputations and actions indicate that he is acting in good faith and not picking brains . . . *and* if the designer is sufficiently experienced to make a realistic estimate, even a speculative bid may be justified.

The rationale of when to bid and when not to bid has, however, been covered in the preceding chapter.

The important point to stress about the fee quoted for a complete installation is that the designer is bound by it and bound also to the concept accepted by the client. The designer is not free to stray from the original outline— partly because it is in the contract, but partly also because any change in the cost basis or increases in the cost due to errors would erode the anticipated profits.

For this reason the dangers of unanticipated costs and expense surprises are the key factors to consider in arriving at a mark-up percentage to produce the necessary profit. Once the contract for installation at a specific total price is signed, the responsibility for the completion of the job rests on the designer's shoulders and pocketbook.

If the design firm has had sufficient experience in the area of work involved—be it hotels, restaurants, lobbies, model builders' development houses, or whatever—to project costs realistically, the turn-key or completed-job basis for arriving at a fee can be very rewarding. It requires a sound knowledge of product availability and of the kind of cooperation which can be expected of suppliers, workshops, artisans, and others whose participation is required, in addition to accuracy and meticulousness in the basic estimating of the complete job.

7. *Other methods*
   The longer a designer works in the non-residential field, the more adept he will become at selecting and applying the fee basis best suited to the needs of the client and the conditions of the job. Among other fee-setting bases which he may learn to apply is the *per square foot charge* for designing and space planning. One firm in the store planning field charges for its services at a rate of approximately seventy cents per square foot of space to be done. Another firm charges for its services in planning and designing office space on the basis of fifty cents per square foot plus a mark-up percentage on purchases.

There is no substitute for analyzing the financial returns earned on completed jobs in the light of the fee requirements of each design firm and the scope of services for each specific job.

Chapter Nineteen

Non-Residential Field—Letter of Agreement

Letters of agreement spelling out the conditions of a job are an absolute necessity in all branches of interior design. Letters of agreement for residential work were studied in Chapter 7. In non-residential work their role is even more crucial, since the client is a business organization with a business approach to every requirement of the job. The business client places stronger emphasis on the exact definition of the designer's performance, on the time sequence of the work, on every budgetary consideration, and on any conditions which may be specific to each job. The design firm must be able to define all of these factors clearly and unequivocally in a letter of agreement that will serve as a proper business instrument.

Basic to preparing the letter of agreement is the accumulation of the facts and conditions of the job. This is easily done if the designer has thoroughly analyzed the job. Again the importance of analyzing the scope of the job must be stressed, and the reader is urged to refer repeatedly to the check lists of points relevant to this analysis which are studied in Chapter 17. There is no way to prepare a satisfactory letter of agreement without it.

As in the residential field, the letter of agreement is prepared and must be signed by both client and design firm before any part of the job is begun. (The only exception to this rule occurs when firms prepare presentations and proposals to bid for the job, a procedure covered in Chapter 17.) The letter of agreement should be prepared after the initial meeting with a potential client and after the client has requested that the designer make a presentation (if that is required) or proceed with the design phase of the job.

The points which the letter of agreement must define are:

1. **The premises.** Their nature and location must be specified, for example: "We are pleased to submit our agreement outlining our proposed work as designers and consultants for your new *offices* (or *hotel* or *restaurant* or whatever) at *6000 Pacific Boulevard.*"

2. **The specific areas involved.** They must be defined in detail. For a hotel, for example, the description should indicate specific public areas such as lobby, lounge, dining room or whatever, special suites and the number thereof, and the number of guest rooms, etc. For an office, the number of private and general offices should be given, and their grouping should be indicated. In any kind of job where identical layouts are to be multiplied—which happens in hotel, motels, offices, and other jobs—the number of times that any layout or scheme is to be repeated should be specified.

3. **The services to be performed,** and the order in which they are to be performed. The various services which the designer will have to render in carrying through the job should be spelled out, and in the proper order, to provide a guide and schedule for both designer and client. Such services might include:

   a. Preparation of a detailed survey or analysis of the program,
   b. Preparation of preliminary layouts for client review,
   c. Preparation of detailed layouts,
   d. Preparation of budgets,
   e. Presentation of purchase recommendations illustrated with photos, sketches, or samples (in the case of fabrics and materials),
   f. Preparation of paint specifications,
   g. Responsibility for the ordering of materials, furnishings, and accessories,

h. Or—preparation of purchase specifications to be used by the client's own purchasing department,

i. Expediting and/or supervising the contractor(s),

j. Expediting and/or supervising the installation.

4. **Defining the Functional and Sequential Phases of the Job.** The different tasks entailed should be organized into logical phases if possible, and it usually is. It is essential if the fee arrangements employ more than one compensation base within one job. For example, if the designing and planning of an office will be charged for on a flat fee, and the purchasing of materials and services will be charged for as a percentage of the cost, it would be necessary to state so in the letter of agreement.

5. **The responsibilities of the client's own contractors.** Whatever work will not be within the scope of the designer's responsibilities should be specified, as well as any occurences or expenses for which he will not be financially liable. Here the designer might specify that:

a. He is not responsible or financially liable for changes made by architects and/or contractors at the client's order.

b. The client is required to give the designer advance notice of any changes he intends to make in the job after he has accepted the designer's proposals.

c. The client is responsible for the provision of storage space for furnishings which arrive at the job site before they can be installed.

d. The client is responsible for the provision of space and facilities for members of the designer's staff who must work at the premises to receive and install furnishings and materials.

6. **The Designer's Fees.** The fee arrangements must be clearly described, both as to the compensation base and the timing of payments. Of course, if the fee will be a flat fee for the whole job, an amount of money will be stated instead of a compensation base. In the case of a flat fee, the statement might read:

Our fee for the above services will be
$...................., *payable as follows:*
$...................., *on signing of this agreement*
$...................., *on acceptance of plans and layouts*
$...................., *on presentation of purchase specifications and requisitions*
$...................., *on installation.*

In the case of fee bases that are to be computed, it is essential, as stated above, to specify the system of computation and the percentage, as well as the timing of payments. The order of payments as the job progresses is an important point to be meticulously specified and meticulously followed. Progress payments should be scheduled to keep up with production costs. A typical example of such a schedule might be:

20% of the fee as a retainer to be paid on the signing of the contract

10% on the approval of design drawings

20% on the receipt of working drawings

10% on the receipt of working schedules and purchasing orders

20% as requested during the progress of construction and installation

115

20% upon completion of scheduled installations.

In addition to the fee, there should be a clear statement on the reimbursement of expenses, such as:

a. travel expenses
b. blueprint costs
c. long-distance telephone charges
d. preliminary concept sketches
e. color renderings
f. time charges for design of custom items
g. other financial liabilities, as:

1. delivery charges
2. sales taxes
3. additional services not covered in the letter of agreement
4. changes made by the client after the designer's proposals have been accepted
5. if the client is doing the purchasing and must turn to the designer for purchasing on items he fails to obtain, the designer shall charge a service charge of ....% for such purchases.

7. **Termination of the Agreement.** The conditions under which the assignment can be terminated should be stated. For example:

"In the event this job is terminated before completion, the retainer fee shall be used as compensation for services rendered. In the event that the cost of such services is less than the retainer, we shall remit the balance to you. In the event that the cost of such services is greater than the retainer, we shall bill you for services rendered at our regular hourly rate."

If merchandise and services are being purchased for the client, there should be a statement of the client's liability for all such orders placed.

The important essential for a good letter of agreement or contractual statement of the services and conditions of a job is a thorough understanding of the job itself. It is recommended that the designer retain an attorney to draw up a contract if complex legal technicalities enter into the conditions of the job. If a contract is prepared by the client's attorney, then the designer should have it reviewed by his own attorney. If a designer is inexperienced in preparing letters of agreement for non-residential work, it is advisable that he ask his attorney to review (if not write) the first few that the designer prepares for non-residential jobs until the designer has enough experience to guide himself.

The examples of actual letters of agreement and statements of services appended here can serve as guides to the various conditions which must be covered and as models for wording and organization:

Letter A covers the development of a design concept for specified areas of a new hotel under construction.

It defines:
1. the specific areas,
2. the data to be delivered to the hotel management, and the form in which the data is to be presented,
3. additional services to be rendered,
4. fees and manner of payment,
5. reimbursement of expenses,
6. responsibilities of the client,
7. additional services,
8. conditions pertaining to the commencement of work and revisions.

LETTER "A"

Client's
Name   **A**
And Address
City

Dear (Client):

This letter will confirm our arrangements in conjunction with
the (   ) Hotel, (   ) ,Bahamas.

The services to be rendered by our firm are outlined as follows:

1. We will design, layout and select furnishings for the
    following:

    HOTEL:

    398 Typical Bedrooms, two (2) color schemes

     21 Typical Parlors, one (1)   "   "
1
      4 Presidential Parlors, one (1) color scheme

      8 Public Corridors, one (1)   "   "

    VILLAS:

      40 Typical Bedrooms, two (2) color schemes
1
      40 Typical Parlors, two (2)   "   "

2. We will prepare two (2) complete color scheme books of typical
    layouts.

3. We will prepare two (2) complete furniture and furnishings
    books.

4. We will prepare two (2) typical layout books.
2
5. We will prepare floor furniture layout plans.

A

-2-

3   6. In conjunction with the aforementioned, we shall select furniture, fabrics (i.e. upholstery, drapery and bedspread) paint colors and/or wall coverings, floor coverings, lighting fixtures, lamps and decorative accessories.

3   7. Consultation and/or selection of color and materials for toilet areas.

3   8. Final inspection of installation

Our fee for the above service shall be $00,000.00, and the schedule of payment shall be:

1. $0,000.00 upon the signing of this letter of agreement.

4   2. $0,000.00 upon approval of layouts, furniture, etc., as enumerated in paragraph #6.

3. $0,000.00 upon your receipt of complete design package as enumerated in paragraphs #2, #3, #4, and #5.

In addition to the above fee, we will bill you monthly for:

1. Out-of-pocket expenses, such as traveling expenses and blueprint cost.

5   2. Black and white preliminary concept sketches $150.00.

3. Color renderings of final concept at $275.00.

4. Any special design furniture, furnishings, etc. shall be billed at our hourly cost.

6   You shall be responsible for specifications, count, purchasing, orderings, receiving and supervision of installation.

7   If the client desires (Interior Design Firm) to render services for any areas not specified in this letter, written agreement shall be made to cover such additional services.

Design services shall commence upon receipt of "Final" construction drawings, i.e. room layouts and details, electric, air-conditioning, T.V. and communications, typical window elevations, and detailed schedule of finishes and materials, etc. This office is to be notified of any and all revisions to above drawings. In the event that revisions are received after your approval of final layouts, and necessitate redesign, (Interior Design Firm) shall be entitled to additional compensation, based upon our hourly cost or other specific costs incurred.

-3-

if the above meets with your approval, kindly sign and return
to us carbon copy attached, together with check as specified
above.

                    Very truly yours,

                    (Interior Design Firm)

ACCEPTED_____   DATE_____

A

B

LETTER "B"

Client's
Name and
Address
City

Dear (Client):

The following is an outline of our scope of services and
method of working for your new plant of the (   )
to be located in (   ).

The AREAS involved will be:

Administrative

Senior Vice-Presidents Office
Junior Vice-Presidents Office
Their Adjacent Secretarial Areas

Class "A"

Advertising Director
Controller
Labor Relations Director
Circulation Director
Public Relations Director
Production Manager

1

Class "B"

General Advertising Manager
Advertising Manager
Retail Advertising Manager
Classified Manager
Circulation Manager
News Editor
Mercury Editor
Budget Officer

Class "C"

Personnel Manager
Chief Accountant
Internal Auditor
Credit Manager

-2-

Class "D"

    Ad Plans Manager
    Copy Service Manager
    Asst. Credit Manager
    Asst. Production Manager

1

    Front Lobby
    Classified Phone Room
    Women's Department
    Food Editor

Conference Rooms

    Advertising
    Labor Relation
    Circulations
    Assembly Room
    Cafeteria

B

The SERVICES we will perform:

2   Preliminary layouts will be made from architect's drawings with floor plans and rough visualization sketches for coordination of our ideas with yourself.

2   Our design would be coordinated with all mechanical requirements such as air conditioning, plumbing, etc.

2   We shall present all design work for review and approval by you in the form of sketches.

2   We will provide photographs of sketches of specific items recommended for purchase.

2   We will prepare paint specifications, charts and color sheets for all interior areas, noting other wall coverings where specified.

3   We will shop for all materials, furnishing and accessories to be used and provide purchasing specifications, schedules, and requisitions for use of your purchasing department or a designated purchasing organization of your choice who will handle all purchasing from this point on through delivery and payment.

2   We will expedite all orders and supervise constructions in collaboration with you, the architect, the building engineers and the contractors of your choice, and provide reasonable

-3-

2

supervision at the proper time of all installation of interior furnishing, labor in placement of furniture, draperies, pictures, accessories, etc. We will attend any necessary conferences such as may be required for the proper development of our work.

B

2

We will supervise and coordinate the final installation in accordance with an estimated time schedule, the deadline of which will be established by you.

4

The CLIENTS/CONTRACTORS RESPONSIBILITIES:

It shall be the contractor's responsibility to inform (Interior Design Firm) of any changes that take place that will affect the work being done by us.

Revisions and changes may be made during the study stages of the work. Changes in completed stages of the work resulting from revised ideas or structural or mechanical exigencies will be made on a time/cost basis. Such changes and revisions will be made upon receipt of your written order.

You shall provide personnel, space and facilities to receive, check, store and place all deliveries.

The FEES for above services:

Our fee for the above services will be $00,000.00, payable as follows:

$0,000.00 on the signing of this agreement

5

$0,000.00 upon acceptance of plans and layouts

$0,000.00 upon presentation of purchase specifi-
                    cations and requisitions.

$0,000.00 on installation

6

The client shall be responsible for all delivery charges and sales taxes where applicable.

6

In addition to the fee, we will bill you monthly at our cost for all necessary blue printing and any other out-of-pocket expenses in this category.

If the client desires (Interior Design Firm) to render services not specified by this contract, written agreement shall be made

—4—

6   to cover such additional services. In the event of extra
drafting time or other expenses incurred by (Interior Design
Firm) due to changes ordered by you after acceptance of original designs and specifications, (Interior Design Firm) will
be entitled to additional compensation based upon our hourly
costs.

6   If requested, we will provide one water color rendering for
Class "A" offices. In the event additional color renderings
or presentations are necessary, such renderings shall be billed
to you at our cost.

B

7   In the event source of supply which we specify will not sell
you directly and you wish (Interior Design Firm) to act as your
purchasing agent, we will handle all such purchasing through
delivery and payment for a service charge of 15 per cent.

8   Notwithstanding the above, it is understood and agreed that
either party may terminate this agreement upon notice to the other.
In the event of such termination, (Interior Design Firm) shall be
entitled to payment for work completed, based on a time charge, as
of the date of termination.

If this agreement meets with your approval, kindly sign and
return to us the enclosed carbon copy of this letter, together with
a check in the amount specified above.

                          Sincerely,

                          (Interior Design Firm)

Enclosure

ACCEPTED BY_____

DATE_____

C

LETTER "C"

Mr. B
President
Address
New York, New York

Dear Mr. B:

This letter will serve as our agreement in outlining the services
to be rendered by (Interior Design Firm) in connection with the
construction and furnishing of new offices at_____Street, New
York City.

In this connection (Interior Design Firm) agrees to perform the
following services:

1. Phase 1

    A. To complete a detailed survey of existing 8th floor
        at the above location.

    B. To prepare a detailed layout of the renovated area
        showing all furniture, equipment and personnel and
        indicating all information required for the develop-
        ment of working drawings.

    C. To prepare a preliminary budget, obtaining such bids
        and developing such estimates as may be required for
        a cost determination, gathering and compiling such
        data as may be required for any final decision.

    D. To prepare those demolition/construction design drawings,
        specifications, and obtain contractors for the bidding
        and completion of the work.

    E. To make such design and color studies as may be necessary
        to reach a final scheme for decorative treatment.

2. Phase II

    A. To select all furniture, draperies, carpets and other
        decorative items, developing full decorative schemes
        for all areas, and after approval, to purchase such
        furnishings on your behalf.

    B. To closely supervise all work in the field to completion
        to ensure adherence to the plans and specifications.

Fees

For the above services, (Interior Design Firm) shall be compensated
as follows:

-2-

3. Phase I

    Our fee shall be computed on the basis of our hourly charges
    for actual time expended by personnel involved. Such time
    charges are calculated at the rate of three times the actual
    hourly base pay, with the exception of (Mr. Blank), whose time
    is charged at an hourly rate of $50.00 All time charges will
    be billed to you monthly.

4. Phase II

    Purchases of furniture, cabinet work, and construction work
    made in your behalf will be billed at our net cost after all
    trade discounts, plus 25%.

5. In addition to the fee, we will bill you monthly at cost for all
    out-of-pocket expenses, such as travel expenses, and for any
    necessary blueprinting.

    You shall be responsible for all delivery charges and sales taxes
    where applicable.

6. In the event extra drafting time, or other expenses are incurred
    by (Interior Design Firm) due to changes ordered by you after ac-
    ceptance of original designs and specification, (Interior Design
    Firm) will be entitled to additional compensation based upon our
    hourly cost, or other specific costs incurred.

7. A retainer fee of $00,000.00, which is required on signing of this
    contract, shall be applied to your account. In the event that this
    job is terminated before completion, the above retainer fee shall
    be used as compensation for services rendered. In the event that
    the cost of such services are less than the retainer, we shall re-
    mit the balance to you. In the event that the cost of such services
    are greater than the retainer fee, we shall bill you for services
    rendered, based upon our cost records.

If the above meets with your approval, kindly sign and return to us
carbon copy attached, together with check as specified above.

                              Very truly yours,

                              (Interior Design Firm)

ACCEPTED_____   DATE_____

C

D

LETTER "D"

Agreement between (Interior Designer) and the (Client).

ARTICLE 1 - SCOPE OF SERVICES:

(Interior Design Firm) will act as designers and consultants on the style and taste of the interior of the areas which include decorations, furnishings, interior architectural details, treatments of walls, floors, ceilings and lighting.

We will collaborate with you as the client, architect and contractor and attend any necessary conferences such as may be required for proper development of the work.

We will take preliminary layouts and we will prepare itemized estimates to be submitted for your approval. In the event additional drawings or renderings other than those originally submitted are requested, an extra charge will be made for each sketch at our actual cost.

We will provide purchasing specifications, schedules and requisitions for the use of your Purchasing Department who will handle all purchasing from this point on through delivery and payment.

We will prepare paint specifications, charts and color sheets for all interior areas, noting other wall coverings. All paint samples <u>must</u> be approved by our office before applying.

We shall present all design work or drawings for review and approval by you in the form of sketches or drawings. We shall also present all selections of furnishings, accessories and interior

-2-

materials for review and approval by you before proceeding with
purchasing. We will provide photographs or sketches of specific
items recommended for purchases if required.

D

ARTICLE 2 - CLIENT/CONTRACTOR RESPONSIBILITIES:

It shall be the client/contractor's responsibility to inform
us of any changes that take place that will affect the work being
done by us.

Revisions and changes may be made during the study stages of
the work. Changes in completed stages of the work resulting from
revised ideas or structural or mechanical exigencies will be made
on a time/charge basis. Such changes and revisions will be made
upon receipt of your written order.

ARTICLE 3 - PHASES OF WORK:

Phase 1 - Development & Detailing of Design Concept:

A - Conferences with executives to determine design
    concept of all individual offices.

B - Detailing of interior architecture in conjunction
    with architects and engineers.

C - **Preparation of** budget estimates for design and
    procurement.

D - Color scheme projection for entire complex.

E - Phasing out of design concept for:

First Floor:
Lobby
Conference area including waiting room, projection
room and two spare offices
Right wing office area

-3-

Second Floor:
Board Room
Mr. Blank's office
Mr. Jones' office
All other private offices
Secretarial banks

D

F - (Client) reserves the right to terminate the
agreement upon submission of the design concept
and upon payment of the fee for phase one.

Phase 2 - Section of all furnishings, accessories and
interior materials. Preparation of purchase specifications
and coordination of purchasing with your Purchasing
Department. Supervision of trade source progress and
completed material. Supervision of installation.

ARTICLE 4 - FEES:

For the above services (Interior Design Firm) shall be

compensated as follows:

Phase 1 - For the development of all design concepts as
outlined above, our fee shall be (   ).

Phase 2 - Our fee for purchasing the materials and services
as will be specified for all areas shall be 20% of the cost
of all actual purchases made as specified in our purchase
requisition.

In addition to the fees outlined above, we will bill you
monthly at our cost for all necessary blueprints and any
other out-of-pocket expenses.

METHOD OF PAYMENT:

Re: Phase 1 - We require one third of our fee upon

acceptance of this agreement, as a retainer to cover the cost of

all preliminary work and to secure our services.

Balance to be paid as follows: One-third at acceptance of

design concept; balance due upon completion of installation.

-4-

Re: Phase 2 - The client shall forward to (Interior Design

Firm) duplicate copies of all source invoices and (Interior Design

Firm) shall bill the client 20% on the cost price of all such

invoices for his services in connection with the buying of such

goods and services.

D

In the event that the client cannot purchase directly from

any indicated sources, (Interior Design Firm) shall be paid a 25%

commission on such purchases and if a deposit is required by the

trade sources, request will be made to the client for such amount

of deposit.

The client shall be responsible for all delivery charges

and sales taxes where applicable. The client shall provide

personnel, space and facilities to receive, check, store and place

all deliveries.

It is agreed that the completion date of March 31st can

be met with all work covered by the project complete and delivered.

If the foregoing meets with your approval, kindly sign

the enclosed copy of this letter and return together with your

check in the amount of (   ).

Very truly yours,

Approved: _____

Date: _____

Letter B covers the development of a design concept and the provision of specifications for materials and furnishings to be purchased by the client's own purchasing department for a new newspaper plant in payment for a flat fee. It defines:

1. the areas,
2. the services to be rendered,
3. the purchasing data and services to be provided by the designer to the client's purchasing department,
4. responsibilities of the client and/or client's contractors,
5. the fee and method of payment,
6. the reimbursement of expenses and additional charges,
7. the basis of charges should the designer do the purchasing,
8. conditions for termination.

Letter C, demonstrates a clear organization of different phases of a job where more than one compensation base is used. In this case there are two distinct phases of work, each with its own compensation base. The points covered are:

1. the services to be rendered in the first phase,
2. the purchasing services comprising the second phase,
3. the fee basis for the first phase,
4. the fee basis for the second phase,
5. reimbursement of expenses, and charges for delivery and sales taxes,
6. responsibility for changes in approved plans,
7. conditions for termination.

Letter D demonstrates an even more highly organized format defining the job scope, the separate phases, and the compensation for each phase, as well as the responsibilities of the client and extra charges. It is hardly necessary to itemize the points included in this agreement since the outline form used in the text of the agreement itself makes these points obvious.

Chapter Twenty

Non-Residential—Estimates and Procedures

In essence the procedures followed in making proposals, estimating, and carrying through non-residential jobs are elaborations and extensions of the procedures for residential work (which were outlined in earlier chapters). The necessity for going into much greater detail in itemizing proposals and in keeping control of the data throughout the progress of the job lies not only in the business client's demand for meticulous accounting, but in the sheer complexity and size of many non-residential jobs, the greater elaboration and originality of the design concepts which are often called for, and the consequently far greater investment in drafting time required for the production of working drawings and details. The control system to be used can be described as an explosion of the procedures outlined in Chapter 25 on the Job Book, except that the drawings, control sheets, and samples may amount to anywhere between ten and thirty times the number of those shown in the residential job book illustrated in that chapter.

In spite of the plethora of individual items, however, the procedures in non-residential work can be boiled down to a logical sequence. Those which follow are systematically used by a New York firm of young and aggressive designers:

1. **Initial Contact with the Client:** This step has been thoroughly discussed in Chapter 17.

2. **Presentation of Theme and Concept:** The firm's presentation consists of the following items:

    a. colored renderings
    b. black and white sketches elaborating on details in the renderings
    c. floor plans with furniture layouts
    d. elevations
    e. paste-up boards presenting photos and/or sketches of furniture and accessories
    f. color-scheme boards with samples of upholstery and drapery materials, carpets, wood finishes, other surfacing materials, and paint colors.

At the presentation meeting the designers describe their concept of a solution for the client's program and requirements as these were defined by the client at the initial meeting. The designers explain the functional rationale of the solution they propose, and relate exactly how they developed the cost figures and budget requirements entailed in their proposals. It is crucial that the designer have the figures at his fingertips. Nothing dooms a presentation more hopelessly than an incomplete grasp of figures. The designer must be absolutely sure of definite figures. Guessing and blustering serve no purpose in a confrontation with businessmen.

At this stage the designer will either obtain the client's approval or be asked to revise his proposals. Where the requested revisions involve functional or budgetary factors, the designer should comply as conscientiously as possible.

3. **Detailing:** After the client approves the proposals, the designers prepare sets of drawings elaborating on the following facets of the job:

    A. Furniture Layout:
    1. A floor plan is drawn of every room, showing furniture in position and drawn to scale,

    2. A code number is assigned to each item and indicated on the drawing,

    3. An inventory list of all the items is prepared. This step of the procedure produces:

    a) A guide for the installation of every room,

and b) a guide for the volume purchasing which can easily be cross-referenced to the purchase orders.

B. Reflected Ceiling Plan:
1. Lighting layout
2. Special ceiling treatment, if any
3. Light fixture coding
4. Inventory of light fixtures

C. Paintings, Wallcovering and Floor Covering allocation:
1. On scaled elevations, every surface of every wall is drawn and lettered to indicate its:

Materials

Decorative accessories—the items and their heights and locations

Wall light fixtures—items, heights, locations

2. Floor information indicates identity and position of carpeting, wood, terrazzo, etc.

D. Shop Drawings
Shop drawings are prepared for the fabrication of every item of special design and custom fabrication. They are always coded back to the original coding indicated on the plan and purchasing specifications.

All materials and paint colors are listed and coded to symbols on plans and elevations. These code symbols are cross-referenced to detail drawings, color code books, and purchasing instructions.

4. **The Color-Scheme Folder:** A sampling of all fabrics, colors, and finishes, and all items are coded to the floor plans and trade source instructions.

5. **The Paint Folder:** illustrates all paint colors, which are coded to the plans and the Paint and Wallcovering allocation.

This procedure is followed for all rooms or, in case of a multiple installation, all scheme variations.

6. **Purchase Sheet and Budget:** The budget and the purchasing sheets are prepared, preferably in book form, starting with the first coded item on the original furniture layout plan. It is of major importance that the same code number be used consistently for every item throughout the work.

The information for purchase requisitions or purchase orders must be broken down for each manufacturer or vendor giving all pertinent data—quantity, description, etc., with the code symbol identifying the item on the original plan.

The form of these purchase sheets depends upon the size and nature of the job. Variations in format are suggested by the illustrative material presented in previous chapters. The illustrated job book and purchasing sheets will serve as a sound base for developing a system to suit the needs of each job.

Purchasing Procedures
The purchasing procedures in major non-residential jobs such as hotels entail enormous responsibility and consequently extremely conscientious attention to detail, because of the tremendous amount of material and money involved. The designer should be particularly alert in adhering to the following principles and practices:

1. Before they are issued, all purchase orders

should be checked as to their conformity with designs, specifications, colors, textures, etc. Any changes initiated by clients must be brought to the attention of the designer, since changes are a potential source of problems in the overall design.

2. Every purchase order should instruct the vendors or manufacturers to mark the outside of all cartons and crates with the code number and the room or space for which the item is destined. The merchandise itself must be marked by affixing a tag or band indicating the same information.

3. Acknowledgement of orders placed must be furnished by the suppier within a reasonable period and indicate:

   a. Delivery date,
   b. Delivery method and route to be used by the supplier.

4. Delivery dates must be constantly reviewed to make sure the various suppliers will deliver on schedule.

5. The receiving clerk or other agency charged with the responsibility for receiving the merchandise and storing it until installation must:

   a. Check all goods for damages or malfunctions immediately upon delivery. If anything is wrong, a claim must be made at once.

   b. Make certain that all goods are properly marked.

   c. Arrange storage so that a proper sequence can be followed for installation purposes.

Estimates

Quite frequently the initial contact with a potential client will result in a request for additional information with regard to the services the designer will render and his concept of a design schedule together with a typical budget estimate. This is quite true when working with clients whose job may be of large scope such as a hotel contemplated or under construction. A request of this nature was made of a design firm who submitted the following information which can serve as a good guide for the reader:

INTERIOR DESIGN FIRM
Address
Telephone

BASE OF OPERATION:

The following outline is prepared as a guide, to illustrate the services
performed by our firm. However, the extent of services can be modified to
accommodate any job situation or requirement. Design concepts and selections
shall be presented, after thorough consultation, for your approval.

DESIGN SERVICES:

1. Prepare for your approval designs, layouts, furniture and furnishings for
    Hotel Rooms, Public Corridors and Elevator Foyers.

2. Prepare for your approval concept renderings of areas under consideration.

3. Specifically, we will select furniture, fabrics, i.e. upholstery, drapery,
    bedspreads, paint colors and/or wallcoverings, floor coverings, lighting
    fixtures, lamps and decorative accessories for your approval.

4. Prepare for quantity take-off and installation, individual floor furniture
    plans, indicating by room numbers, a count schedule, coded color schemes,
    and paint/wallcovering allocation.

5. Prepare for purchasing and installation typical room and suite floor plans,
    color schemes, and picture installation elevations. This information is
    presented in bound book form.

6. Prepare for purchasing and job record, furniture and furnishings books,
    pictorially illustrating those items, including specifications, disposition,
    upholstery and finish. This information is presented in bound book form.

7. We will inspect all furniture and furnishings either in production, phototypes
    or shop drawings as required.

8. We will coordinate with building architect regarding material and color
    selections for toilets, dressing areas, corridors and elevator lobbies.

9. We shall periodically inspect installation as required.

REMUNERATION

1. Will be a design fee, which is based on amount of time to perform the
    required services.

2. Out-of-pocket expenses directly associated with the execution of this
    commission, shall be reimbursed.

3. Concept renderings shall be billed to you at our cost.

PURCHASING

1. We will prepare purchase orders on your stationery, which will be returned
    to you for your review, authorization, deposit (if necessary) and issuance
    to vendor.

2. Each purchase order prepared by this office shall contain in addition to
    quantity, specifications, etc., containing marking instructions to facilitate
    installation.

3. For the preparation of purchase orders we shall be remunerated on a fee basis.

CLIENT RESPONSIBILITY

1. Selection of a receiving agent who will receive, inspect, store and install
    furnishings.

2. Coordinator who will act as liaison and prepare site installation, schedule
    and coordinate with receiving agent.

3. Payment of all vendors bills.

4. Payment of receiving agent, storage and installation costs.

SCHEDULE 2

PAGE 1

Prepared by
Interior Design Firm

PROPOSED DESIGN SCHEDULE

| FLOORS | DESIGN PERIODS | COLOR SCHEDULES | | ROOM TYPE | | | TOTAL ROOMS |
	-	L.R.	B.R.	LANAI	L.R.	B.R.	-
Lanai	1	1	-	9	0	0	9
2nd Floor	1	1	2	0	4	29 (2 alcoves)	33
3rd Floor	Same as 2nd Floor	Same as 2nd Floor	Same as 2nd Floor	0	2	31	33
4th Floor	1	1	2	0	2	31	33
5th Floor	Same as 4th Floor	Same as 4th Floor	Same as 4th Floor	0	2	31	33
6th Floor	1	1	2	0	2	31	33
7th Floor	Same as 6th Floor	Same as 6th Floor	Same as 6th Floor	0	2	31	33
8th Floor Upper/Lower							
Town House Suites	Same as 2nd Floor	Same as 2nd Floor	Same as 2nd Floor	0	14	14	28
Royal Suite	1	1	2	0	1	2	3
Deluxe Suites	Same as 4th Floor	Same as 4th Floor	Same as 4th Floor	0	6	12	18
Special Suites	Same as 6th Floor	2	3	0	2	3	5
Total Design Periods	5						
Total Color Schemes		8	11				
Total Room Types				9	37	215	
Total Rooms							261

SCHEDULE 3

PAGE 1

Prepared by
Interior design firm

PROPOSED FURNISHINGS BUDGET FOR
TYPICAL LIVING ROOM (TOWN HOUSE SUITES)

Carpet 50 yds.	$8.00		$400.00	
Lining 50 yds.	1.50		75.00	
Labor 50 yds.	2.00		100.00	
		Carpet Total		$ 575.00

One 60" sofa		200.00
Fabric for above 12 yds.	$ 4.50	54.00
Three Lounge chairs	125.00	375.00
Fabric for above 18 yds.	4.50	81.00
Two End tables	60.00	120.00
One Occasional table		50.00
One Credenza		175.00
One Dining/Game Table		100.00
Four Side chairs	75.00	300.00
Fabric for above 4 yds.	4.50	18.00
One Mirror		90.00
Five Pictures		170.00
One table lamp		50.00
Three lamps	30.00	90.00

One pair of draperies, 10 widths wide
Milium lined, labor, hardware and installation   105.00
Fabric for above 40 yds.   120.00

One pair of under-curtains 11 widths wide,
Labor, hardware and installation   69.50
Fabric for above 44 yds.   .95   41.00

One Soft valance, milium lined, labor, hardware
and installation   110.00
Fabric for above 18 yds.   3.00   54.00
                                                     $2,948.50

NOTE: The above does not include
        Shipping charges
        Travel Expenses

SCHEDULE 4

PAGE 1

Prepared by
Interior design firm

PROPOSED FURNITURE BUDGET FOR
TYPICAL BEDROOM

Carpet 42 yds.	$8.00		$336.00	
Lining 42 yds.	1.60		68.00	
Labor 42 yds.	2.00		54.00	
		Carpet Total		$ 458.00
Two 39" headboards			50.00	100.00
Two Carriers			6.75	13.50
Two 39" x 80" box spring & mattress			43.70	87.40
One Night table				60.00
Two Lounge chairs			125.00	250.00
Fabric for above 12 yds.			4.50	54.00
One 48" desk				110.00
One Desk chair with arms				75.00
Fabric for above 1 yd.				4.50
One Table lamp				50.00
One Night table lamp				30.00
One Desk lamp				30.00
Six pictures				150.00
Two Bedspreads:				
Labor to make spread and dust ruffle			40.00	80.00
Fabric for above 26 yds.			3.00	78.00
One pair of draperies, 10 widths wide				
Milium lined - labor, hardware and installation				105.00
Fabric for above 40 yds.			3.00	120.00
One pair of under-curtains - 11 widths wide				
Labor, hardware and installation				9.50
Fabric for above 40 yds.			.95	41.80
One soft valance, Milium lined,				
Labor, hardware and installation				110.00
Fabric for above 18 yds.			3.00	54.00
				$2,155.70

NOTE: The above does not include:
       Built-in chest
       Shipping charges
       Travel expenses

Part 4 Forms, Techniques, and Special Factors

Chapter Twenty-One

Contract Breakdown

The formal written instrument which defines and records the scope of the job, the precise responsibilities of designer and client, and the financial arrangements is the *letter of agreement* or professionally prepared contract described in Chapter 7.

To abide by its numerous provisions requires constant re-reading and referral—a job which is not only time-consuming but also unsatisfactory, since even the greatest alertness cannot insure some costly lapse, a nerve-racking possibility. To avoid such uncertainties and time-consuming effort, a form called a Contract Breakdown should be used. It enables the firm to keep all pertinent details of the letter of agreement readily accessible and clearly defined, and also makes it possible to keep track of progress as each phase of the job is carried out, so that nothing is forgotten or overlooked.

The Contract Breakdown form here reproduced twice is the one used in the office of Melanie Kahane Associates, Inc., New York; it has stood the test of many years' application to a broad variety of jobs. A study of its provisions and of the completed form will indicate why it is worth the time to prepare it.

Before analyzing the information to be entered into the Contract Breakdown, let us note who performs the task, how many copies are made, and who receives the copies. It is either the principal of the firm or the individual responsible for negotiating the arrangements with the client who analyzes and breaks down the provisions of the Letter of Agreement, setting forth each provision in the Contract Breakdown form. The typed copies are duplicated in sufficient number for distribution to:

1. **The Principal**—for observation and handy referral.

2. **The Job Captain** supervising the job and/or **The Job Designer**—to inform them of all pertinent facts of the agreement with the client. This guidance alerts them to the need of promptly recording the time and expenses put into the job, and enables them to phase out the tasks and areas comprising the job as each is completed. This breakdown of the component parts of the job is particularly invaluable if the job designer is responsible for controlling the cost of the job.

3. **The Bookkeeping Department**—for the control of billing and pricing. In some organizations the designer may do the pricing and the bookkeeping department the checking. But more often the bookkeeping department will do the pricing; a Contract Breakdown will give them all the information necessary to perform this task efficiently.

4. **The Secretary** or similar executive-level employee(s) (depending upon the size and administrative organization of the firm).

The one or two-man firm will find the Contract Breakdown invaluable as a basic working tool to control the flow of information needed for the routine execution of all phases of each particular job. The maintenance of either a ready reference file of contract breakdowns of jobs in work or else the keeping of a contract breakdown in each client's job folder takes the guesswork out of the working arrangements.

Information to be Recorded
1. Job Number—if the firm uses job numbers.

2. Client's name and current address.

3. New address—the premises where the work is being done if the client is to move there at the completion of the job.

A

Contract Breakdown Form

Job No. ①	Bill to:	Sp. Notes	Dept. Head ⑦
Name: ②	Name: ④		Deposit ⑧ Rcvd.
Add:	Add:		
	Duplicate P.O. ⑤		Confirmations — Yes ⑨ No
New Add: ③	Spl. Notes		Date of Contract ⑩
	⑥		Time Chge. Limit ⑪ Hrs.
			Exp. Billing ⑫
Duplicate P. O.			Breakdown Apprvd. ⑬

Phase	Area	Scope of Work	Time Charges		Fees	Comm.	Out of Pocket			
			Mk.	St.			Trav.	Subs.	Toll	Bl. Pr.
⑭	⑮	⑯	⑰	⑰	⑱	⑲		⑳		

Form No. 13 (To obtain forms, see page 10.)

B

Contract Breakdown Form

Job No.	Bill to:	Sp. Notes	Dept. Head
Name:	Name:		
Add:	Add:	1–Confirmations requesting deposits required on all purchases (other than fabrics, accessories, etc).	Deposit _____ Rcvd.
	Duplicate P.O.	2–$5,000.00 minimum expenditure on contract.	Confirmations — Yes X No
New Add:	Spl. Notes	3–Deposit of $1,000.00 is applicable to final bill if purchases exceed $5000.	Date of Contract
			Time Chge. Limit _None_ Hrs.
			Exp. Billing _Yes/Monthly_
Duplicate P. O.			Breakdown Apprvd.

Phase	Area	Scope of Work	Time Charges		Fees	Comm.	Out of Pocket			
			Mk.	St.			Trav.	Subs.	Toll	Bl. Pr.
I	ALL	Complete scaled layouts of furniture - to be approved by client. (NOTE: furniture layouts only)	NO	NO			Yes		Yes	.50¢ ea.
II	ALL	Purchases (other than floor coverings)	NO	NO	Retail					
III	ALL	Carpets & other floor coverings	NO	NO		25%				
IV	ALL	Interior painting (including schedules & supervision of all final coats)	NO	NO		15%				
V	ALL	Selection or specification of materials, equipment, hardware etc. as required for kitchens, pantries & bath.	NO	NO		15%				
VI	ALL	1 – Work executed by others but designed, detailed, selected or approved by_____ a–construction b–architectural alterations c–cabinet work	35.00	18.50						
		2 – Consultation with contractors or sub-contractors	35.00	18.50						
		3 – Designing specifications re: all construction or architectural work and alterations.								

4. Name and address of client for billing purposes (Bill to: Name: Address:), with a notation of who is to receive the invoices and where they are to be forwarded.

5. Duplicate Purchase Orders—notation as to whether the client or another designated individual will require duplicate purchase orders.

6. Special Notes or Requirements:
   a. Deposit information pertaining to confirmations.
   b. Contract minimum or information on the budget.
   c. Disposition of original deposit—whether refundable, applicable to purchases or to a fee, etc.
   d. Any other information for the guidance of the principal, the staff, or the bookkeeping department not indicated elsewhere on the form.

7. Name of department head, job captain, or other individual in charge of the job.

8. Deposit—the amount of the required initial deposit and whether it has been received.

9. Confirmations—are they to be sent to clients before the ordering of merchandise and services?

10. Date of Contract or Letter of Agreement.

11. Time-Charge Limit—if the contract has a time-charge element, this notation indicates whether there is a limit to the number of hours that will be paid for, and if so what it is, or whether all chargeable time expended will be charged.

12. Expense Billing—indicates whether the client is to be billed for expenses and the billing frequency.

13. Breakdown approval—after the contract breakdown is analyzed and prepared, it should be checked for correctness by the principal or other authorized individual.

14. Phase Number—to identify each separate phase of the job. Often the letter of agreement establishes the phase breakdown, and this column conforms.

15. Area—for further control of the charges, the specific area of the job to which each item pertains is identified here.

16. Scope of Work—description of details to which various charges pertain.

17. Time charges made for—
    PR—principal
    ST—member of staff

    These two columns indicate which phases of the work will be charged for on a time basis, and show the hourly rates for the principal and the staff.

18. Fees—this column indicates the fee basis for each particular type of work.

19. Comm—this column notes the phases of work which are subject to either commissions or mark-ups, and the rates to be charged.

20. Out of Pocket—recording job expenses such as for travel, subsistence, tolls, and blueprints, and whether the client will or will not be charged for them.

A study of Exhibit B, a completed contract breakdown, illustrates the simplicity of its format combined with its clarity as a capsule checklist enabling a busy office to control a job program through the routinized flow of information to all members of the responsible staff.

Chapter Twenty-Two

The Relationship with Trade Sources

In the past, the three parties involved in the making of an interior were *the patron, the artisan,* and *the interior designer*—who was called something else—perhaps artist-decorator like Louis Comfort Tiffany, or architect like the Adams brothers, or cabinet-maker like Thomas Chippendale. The designer executed virtually everything he designed: what his own workroom couldn't produce—for instance the rugs—he did not discuss with the patron.

Today the three principals are *the client, the trade sources,* and *the interior designer*. The most striking change has been the development of what we call the trade sources—that plethora of manufacturers, wholesalers, dealers, service craftsmen, and contractors geared to work in tandem with interior designers primarily or exclusively (the ideal). They supply the manufactured or custom-made furniture, fabrics, floor coverings, accessories, lamps, lighting fixtures; they sew the draperies; they upholster; they apply fireproofing and other protective treatments to fabrics and dye them; they do the carpentry, the painting, the electrical wiring; they install the floor-coverings—and so forth. They, in short, account for the fact that the design firm with extensive workshops of its own has become the exception rather than the rule. After he leaves the drawing board, the typical interior designer of today behaves more like a purchaser and specifier and less like a producer than in the past—though he produces *custom* results—individualized interiors. The surprising speed with which he can do this depends on the flexibility and efficiency with which the designers and the trade sources have learned to work with each other.

Each design firm has to establish working relationships with the trade sources, on its own, in accordance with the customs of the field, which have evolved for good and sufficient reasons. The nature and importance of that relationship is significantly affected by the geographic location of the designer's firm and the kind of sources he uses.

For the trade sources are not distributed evenly throughout the country; they tend to be concentrated in a few major market centers. The recent acceleration in the growth of the older market centers and deliberate organization of a few newer ones in the past dozen years are impressive clues to the growth of what we might call the interiors industry. The most important of these centers are in New York, Chicago, Los Angeles, San Francisco, Dallas, Atlanta, and Miami. They consist of convenient clusters of showrooms displaying every conceivable type of furnishings for the interior design market.

Designers based within a few hours of such centers enjoy tremendous advantages and conveniences:

1. Continual and effortless awareness of new trends and products,

2. Relative freedom from dependence upon their own stocks of samples and their own library of catalogs and manufacturers' literature,

3. Ease in comparative shopping on prices as well as on product availability,

4. Freedom from the need for costly, time-consuming travel with or without clients to research the market for specific jobs,

5. A wealth of custom manufactures and services such as fabric workrooms and cabinetmakers to choose from close at hand,

6. Lower freight and delivery charges.

Designers far from major market centers must operate a little differently:

1. They must maintain and absorb the cost of more inclusive libraries of samples, catalogs, and manufacturers' reference material.

2. They are more apt to find it convenient to carry an inventory of floor samples and even stock, which in turn can lead naturally into a retail business conducted with interior design service, rather than an interior design operation alone.

3. They should travel periodically to market centers to keep in touch with trends and new products.

4. Because of the additional expenses entailed by the foregoing, they should be careful to choose fee bases and mark-ups which cover the extras realistically.

In developing a working relationship with trade sources, the designer should be aware of the following factors: CREDIT, PURCHASING INFORMATION, and whether the trade source operates a "CLOSED SHOWROOM."

Credit

Without credit, the lifeblood of our economy would cease to flow, for credit is the network of vessels which enables the sustaining fluid of goods and services to move. The practice of interior design is no exception to our universal dependence on credit. The designer extends credit to his clients, and in order to do so needs credit from his trade sources. Their willingness to extend it and under what terms, is based upon his ability to establish a credit standing when he is starting in business, and upon his ability to maintain a rating afterward.

Credit is established through:

1. Registering with the three credit agencies (listed below) and
2. Establishing a good record in trade relations.

1. **The Three Credit Agencies Are:**
   a. **Dun & Bradstreet.** The best known and most universally used source of credit information, it maintains current credit information on all types of businesses.

   b. **Lyon Furniture Mercantile Agency.** This credit agency is best known for its impact in the furniture world. It is used intensively and primarily for organizations that operate shops and maintain inventory. It also registers interior designers and is used as a source of financial information by the manufacturers and managers of wholesale showrooms.

   c. **Allied Board of Trade,** which terms itself "the official registration and credit bureau for the Decorative Furniture Manufacturers' Association and as a credit center for the Drapery, Upholstery, and Allied Decorative Trades." It concerns itself only with the interior design field, and to that purpose:

   1. Publishes its Credit Green Book, which lists the names of approximately 12,000 active designers and summarizes each one's financial condition and suggested credit. This credit Green Book is used by the sources as a handy credit guide and also, to some extent, to verify a prospective purchaser's claim that he is in fact a professional interior designer.

   2. Issues to each listed designer an identification card which assits in identifying the designer to trade sources.

3. Issues other pertinent information to the field in general, and provides direct-mail service for a fee.

The Allied Board of Trade, unlike the other two agencies, has restrictive provisions for registration, to assure the trade to some extent that the designers listed have given proof of:

a. meeting minimum professional standards for scholastic training,

b. meeting minimum professional standards for practical training and experience,

c. being in business:
1. A record of past trade relations,
2. A sales tax number (if in a sales tax area),
3. Stationery, billheads, office forms.

Registration with any of the credit agencies gives the trade sources a quick reference on which to answer a designer's request for credit. New design organizations, especially those in major market centers, may find it very helpful to register with the Allied Board of Trade; its identification cards are particularly useful in opening the doors of showrooms, since they are accepted as definite proofs that the designers holding them are producing members of the profession.

A designer's failure or inability to provide reassuring financial information to the trade source may force him to purchase goods for a client on a C.O.D. basis, or to order custom-made items pro-forma, or to leave large deposits.

Beginners may find themselves having to do any or all of these things to get themselves started, working at first with a limited number of sources until those sources begin to extend credit to them. The next step is to use those sources as a credit reference in applying for credit to new sources. This brings us again to our second method for establishing credit:

2. **Establishing a Good Record in Trade Relations.** The designer who pays trade source bills promptly will find that the fact is readily disclosed to new sources who inquire about him. A poor record leaps through the grapevine even faster. In other words, the designer's record and his rating are identical. It should perhaps be mentioned that credit is not the only thing the designer can lose when his rating drops. He also falls to the bottom of the list for every kind of service and courtesy—the placing of orders, deliveries, adjustments. The designer who pays his bills promptly is assured not only of credit but of the little extra attentions and considerations which oil the wheels of his operation. Maintaining a good credit rating pays dividends.

Purchasing Information

One of the most crucial necessities for a happy relationship between designers and trade sources is clarity in the purchase orders and specifications, so that such matters as dimensions, completion and delivery dates, and other facts needed for the satisfactory manufacture and delivery of the order are not subject to misinterpretation. The factors involved with the relaying of purchasing information are:

1. Purchase Orders
2. Other Specifications
3. Consultations with Craftsmen
4. Changes in Purchase Specifications
5. Adjustments
6. Delivery

1. **Purchase Orders:** The use and preparation of purchase orders was covered in Chapter 13. To restate the basic principle: it is essential to clearly identify the item to be bought and to clearly describe what is to happen to it. If this is done, the designer *must* expect the source to deliver properly or else be accountable for mistakes. Proper purchase orders eliminate one of the most annoying sources of irritation in the field.

2. **Other Specifications—including measurements, working drawings, etc.:** In major market centers it is unusual to find a designer operating even his own drapery workshop, and even in more isolated locations, it is rare to find a design organization completing all its work as a self-contained unit with its own craftsmen. Even where the designer controls the work in his own shop, a proper work program requires that care in making and checking specifications is essential. But it is much more essential when the orders will go to many outside workshops. In such cases something else is essential beside clarity in the measurements and specifications: it is also essential that orders and items be clearly identified and keyed in, since each shop —the contractor, the carpenter, the painter, the electrician, the cabinetmaker, upholsterer, etc. —is always awash with orders from many different designers.

3. **Consultations with Craftsmen:** The designer should avail himself of the craftsman's ability in estimating the cost of special work. This will eliminate disagreements resulting from price surprises caused by unanticipated labor factors discovered in jobs after they have been completed. Similarly, the designer should consult with the craftsman or technician on preparing specifications properly if he has any doubts in such areas as construction details, drapery measurements, electrical work, or the like. Cooperating in advance prevents the discovery of problems after it is too late.

4. **Changes in Purchase Specifications:** Changes in job site conditions which may develop as a project moves along occasionally necessitates changes in purchase orders and specifications already placed with a source. A designer cannot expect the source to bear the resulting financial burden (and he has protected himself from the costs of changes if he has taken proper care with his letter of agreement or contract, as covered in Chapters 7 and 10.). But the source can help the designer in expediting such changes. Where the source has not yet begun to process the order, there should be no penalty to any member of the eternal triangle—designer, client, source. If changes are called for as a result of measurements or specifications computed by the source, there should be no question but that the liability lies with the source. If changes are called for as a result of the source's incorrect interpretation of properly prepared specifications, there should again be no question but that the liability lies with the source. In the last two cases, it is up to the source to make good at its own expense.

5. **Adjustments:** In the preceding paragraph the designer's dependence on the source for assistance in adjusting to changes in the premises has been mentioned. Here the subject is financial adjustments called for by imperfections or inadequacies in the product supplied by the source. If such inadequacies become apparent, the designer has the right to expect his source to cooperate toward an equitable settlement. In this respect it is pertinent that the good, prompt-paying customer will find his source more responsive. It should also be mentioned that the

designer should be aware of cases where the source properly gives formal notification that it does not guarantee the performance of certain goods from the standpoint of durability or similar factors; such disclaimers frequently appear on the tags of luxurious but fragile fabrics.

6. **Delivery:** The timing of delivery is one of the essential factors in a successful installation. The adherence to delivery dates by sources has long been a nettlesome problem. Generally the client specifies an installation date when client and designer agree to proceed with the job, and it is good business to meet this date or come reasonably close to it. As to the role of the sources in making it possible for the designer to meet the installation date by delivering their orders on time, there is no doubt that complications can and do arise which make it impossible for the source to meet a promised date; this is understandable. It also happens, however, that certain sources glibly give assurances about dates when they know that their backlog or other conditions will prevent timely delivery. It is imperative that as he learns by experience, the designer avoid sources which are unreliable in this respect. It is better to work with a source which realistically gives a later date and lives up to it than with a source that will promise anything to get the order and then leave the designer out on a limb, with a frustrated client threatening to saw off that limb.

The Closed Showroom

To repeat: the growth of concentrated showroom centers where trade sources present a tremendous array of merchandise to the professional interior designer is an effect of the tremendous social and economic role which the professional has assumed. As a stimulus to sales and to the designer's imagi-

nation—and certainly as a convenience—the manufacturers' and representatives' showrooms in these concentrated centers are an enormous boon to all concerned, but not an unmitigated boon. Such centers, often easily accessible from the street, attract swarms of non-professional gatecrashers and bargain-hunting types of many kinds.

The undesirables range from clients who intend to beat down their interior designers on mark-ups (after picking their brains) to the hungry, marginal pseudo-professional five-or-ten-percenters, who, having no valid design skills to offer, attempt to exist by acting as shoppers for a subnormal profit. Most of them would be haunting the retail stores today as they used to twenty years ago, if the professional interior design market had not taken the initiative in quality interiors. And like bargain hunters in retail stores, they divert attention and personnel from the bonafide professionals out of all proportion to the size of their potential purchases. For this reason alone the prestigious showrooms regard them as a nuisance. When business is slow, however, some of the marginal showrooms are unwilling to turn out a potential customer, with the result that elevators and corridors of showroom buildings are sometimes crowded to the point where the real pros operate with diminished efficiency. Even worse, as the gatecrashers discuss mark-ups, an undignified and unbusinesslike atmosphere takes over entire showrooms.

Since the qualified designer must protect the professionalism of the field, he would do well to give careful consideration to the practices of the showrooms he intends to patronize. The "open" showroom which welcomes all with only the most perfunctory check of each customer's credentials should be by-passed.

Alive to the dangers of the open showroom, three

professional organizations—the A.I.D., the N.S.I.D., and the Decorators Club have made a united effort to win the showroom managers' cooperation in following a closed showroom policy. In a letter addressed to those in the New York metropolitan area last September (1967), the trade relations committees of these three organizations suggested that each showroom:

"I. Require each visitor to register, prohibiting admission to any member of the public unless accompanied by an accredited interior designer or an accredited architect or unless such visitor presents a specific communication (not just a business card or letterhead) to you from such an accredited interior designer or an accredited architect requesting that the courtesy of your establishment be extended to such visitor.

"II. Effect sales and bill only to accredited interior designers, accredited architects, recognized dealers, or other proper trade purchasers.

"III. Prohibit unbusinesslike conduct by any persons at your premises and particularly discourage any open discussion of trade discounts afforded by you by anyone. Any persons violating this requirement should be required to desist or to leave the premises. Your own personnel should be instructed to discuss discounts only with trade purchasers and never in the presence of members of the public.

"IV. Prohibit the admission of children under twelve or animals.

"V. Particularly if you are located in a showroom, or resource building, join with the other firms located therein in an effort to have the owner or management of your building prohibit access to the building to anyone except persons having spe-

cific business therein. This will prevent the casual shopper and the bargain-hunters from wasting your receptionist's time and otherwise getting underfoot at your premises.

"We appreciate that in order to make such a program effective, it requires the cooperation of a substantial segment of the firms active in our industry. But we also believe that those firms participating will, as a result, enjoy more business with greater profit. Traffic at participating resources will be more meaningful, will be easier to service, and will be of a caliber that will result in greater sales.

"We are certain that members of the interior design profession, whether members of our groups or not, will be substantially influenced to patronize the firms participating in this program by virtue of the very business atmosphere that will be created."

Which just about sums up the mutual interdependence of the profession and the trades, and why they have everything to gain by mutual cooperation in sound business conduct.

Chapter Twenty-Three

The Theory, Objectives, and Method of Recording Time

Though the interior designer appears to be engaged in the sale of tangible merchandise—furnishings, accessories, and so on—this, of course, is not what he sells in actuality. Every sale or purchasing suggestion depends upon the professional competence and time needed to bring the tangible item into focus for an interior which the designer is producing, and the commodities which the *designer* sells are intangibles—*talent* (with the other components of professional competence) and *time*. These commodities are hardly easy to measure in terms of dollar compensation. It is in fact impossible for the writer to suggest a formula for arriving at a just price for professional proficiency. But it is not impossible to find ways of measuring time and of computing its value.

The attitudes about the usefulness of recording time which prevail today among interior designers seem to follow three distinct motivational patterns:

1. Where designers are accustomed to billing their clients for time, the need for a time-recording system is taken as a matter of course.

2. Where designers are attuned to the idea of using statistical information about their own practice for future guidance, the need for a time-recording system is also taken as a matter of course.

3. The third attitude is that of the designers who see no need at all for maintaining time records. This group constitutes the vast majority of designers heading small or one-man organizations. Such firms as a rule give little or no consideration to time as a component of the costs which the firm invests in a job. Their typical procedure on a residential job is to work on a retail or mark-up basis without thought to the relationship of the time spent on the job to the profit that results. They do not ask themselves what the earnings represent in terms of time expended. Did they work for one dollar an hour, five dollars an hour, or what? They do not relate the time eaten up by difficult or garrulous clients to their profit margins. This attitude is both unbusinesslike and unprofessional. It takes intelligence to run a practice successfully, and this intelligence has to be applied to a shrewd study of all the big and little wheels that make an office tick.

The recording of time is an important factor to consider because the information it yields enables a firm to:

1. **Relate Time to Quoting a Fee Basis for a New Job:**
   If time records of previous jobs have been kept, they will indicate the amount of time needed to complete a variety of jobs under a variety of conditions resulting in a variety of profit margins. Assume, for example, that a potential client appears with modest budgets to do three rooms. With the budget as a base, the designer can roughly determine the size of the possible gross profit. By checking back to previous jobs, the designer can estimate how many hours this kind of job has required in the past. Then, by dividing the average number of hours into the average gross profit, he can determine what approximate hourly return he can expect and whether to take the job or not. Similarly, if a potential client wishes to work on a flat-fee basis, the designer can refer to the results of previous jobs, find jobs with a reasonable degree of similarity in salient characteristics, and quote a fee estimate that makes sense.

2. **Relate time to the progress of each current job:**

A periodic review of the time being spent on current jobs can be revealing eye-openers on profitable and unprofitable procedures. With an estimate of the predictable gross profit of any given job based upon an analysis of its scope made when he accepts it, the designer is in a position to know how much time it pays him to give the client. If the time records indicate an abnormal consumption of time because of a difficult client personality, they cue the designer to inform the client that either

1) time must no longer be wasted, or

2) the designer will begin to charge extra for the excess time expended in the job. As a matter of fact some design firms provide routinely for the shilly-shally hazard when they quote a retail or mark-up basis for the fee on a residential job. They accomplish this by adding a notation that this fee basis allows a specific number of shopping hours, and that if additional hours are required, they will be charged to the client at an hourly rate. The system is an excellent deterrent to the wasting of valuable time by hemming and hawing clients, and illustrates the value of recording time even in residential work where fees are based upon the cost of merchandise.

The same principle of relating time to the progress of current jobs applies to jobs taken on a flat-fee basis. It is essential that the designer keep a record of time expended as he progresses with the job. Should conditions arise that slow his work either on the drawing board, or in discussions with the client or workmen, or in the solution of problems of installation or delivery, keeping tabs on time used up will prevent him from losing track of the situation and alert him early enough that he must speed up some of the work if he is to avoid an inadequate hourly return on the job. Peculiarly enough, this kind of information is relatively more beneficial to the smaller designer than the one whose firm is larger. Unproductive or wasted time is more apt to occur during the progress of the jobs done by the designers whose staffs are small or consist of themselves alone—the designers who can least afford to waste their energy.

3. **Relate Time to the Completed Job and the Profit Earned Therefrom:**
It has been suggested in previous chapters that jobs can very easily be analyzed for costs, selling price, and gross profits through the maintenance of some form of inventory control sheet. If the designer also maintains a time record for each job, he will have an immediate picture available showing the relationship of the profit to the time expended. This information can then be related to:

1. The hourly return earned,
2. the design firm's ability to complete a job profitably,
3. the productivity of individual staff members, and
4. the establishment of a record of job costs and profits to be used for future guidance.

4. **Relate Time to the Billing to be Made Against a Client if the Letter of Agreement Calls for Such Charges:**
If the working arrangements with a client call for any type of time-charge billing, it is imperative that time records be maintained with accuracy. This is necessary not only for the primary purpose of accumulating time for billing to the client, but for providing corroborative information in the event time charges are questioned. It can be taken for granted that some-

153

where in the progress of a job in which time is a billing factor, the client will question the charges. The designer must be in a position to substantiate the time billing by referring to time records which will indicate the date, the number of hours expended, and a description of the services performed.

5. **Relate Time to the Productivity and Activities of Employees:**
By the very nature of his work, the typical interior designer must move about a great deal, visiting clients, job sites, the workshops where craftsmen must be supervised, and, of course, shopping. Design firms which employ staff designers must maintain a reasonable degree of control over the activities of such employees. A review of their activities will indicate the productivity of individual employees as well as the relative profit importance of various activities. Since employee salaries are a major item in the overhead of a design office, it is essential to relate the cost of an employee to his productivity. Many firms consider the observation of employee activities with deep concern, and maintain records of each employee's income productivity along with his time productivity, periodically reviewing them for profitability and efficiency.

Valuation of Time
If time billing is to be a factor in an interior designer's fee basis, and if time recording is to be a factor in maintaining statistical and historical records, then a dollar basis for charging time must be developed. The cost basis for time charges breaks down into two distinct categories:

1. *The charge for the principal's time*
2. *The charge for employees' time*

1. **The Charge for the Principal's Time.**
The time charge for the principal of a firm or for an individual interior designer practicing alone must be evaluated differently from the time charge for an employee. The following factors must be considered in arriving at the time charge for the principal or lone designer:

1. *Geographic location*
The geographic region where the designer's office is located has a bearing upon the attitude of clients towards time charges. In some parts of the country a charge of about $25 per hour is taken by clients in stride; in other areas clients look askance at such a rate, and indeed at the idea of time charges in itself.

2. *Economic status of clients*
The economic habits, standard of living, and financial resources of the clients and their community and social circle have a decided bearing both on the size of time rates and on the use of time charges.

3. *Availability*
The availability of the designer to accept work has a tremendous bearing on what he computes to be the value of his time. The designer who is in demand can certainly think in terms of a much higher hourly time rate than the designer who is "hungry" for work.

4. *Competition*
The time charges customarily set by competing designers in the same operating area will affect the terms which any designer can safely demand without risking the loss of his potential clients.

5. *Anticipated earnings*
Designers with little confidence in their poten-

tial earnings are happy to make any little "something" by way of income, while others will set their goals to derive what they consider a decent income and adjust their time charges accordingly. Along the same lines, the designer must keep his overhead expenses in proportion to his anticipated earning capacity.

There is no arbitrary formula or rule of thumb that can be counted on to build a chart of time charges for any given designer. However, information for guidance in finding the most advantageous acceptable charge can be derived through:

1. An analysis of the conditions set forth above.

2. The maintenance of time records to cover all types of work performed by the designer, and a comparison between the time expended for each job and the profit earned in it. From this, the value of time for different kinds of jobs can be computed.

3. A calculation of how much needs to be earned in order to cover overhead and the designer's income. For example: If, in a one-man firm, the annual overhead is $10,000 (per year, of course) and the designer sets $15,000 as his annual income, and if one assumes, as is customary, that a principal has about 1,500 productive hours a year, a rate of between $16 and $17 per hour is derived (by dividing 1,500 hours into $25,000). This figure should be compared to the study of the results of earlier jobs described in Item #2 above.

The figure of $25 an hour seems to have become commonly accepted as a base rate in the course of professional conferences among interior de-

signers, perhaps through sheer repetition. This rate should not be used blindly, however. It is always essential to review the factors itemized above.

The principals in our larger design organizations can set any hourly charges they feel is compatible with their reputation, availability, and the type of client to be billed. Principals in the larger firms have many duties other than designing to perform, and each man's time may be divided into many areas. Thus, there is no formula that would make sense in determining all charges. Most nationally known designers work on a basis of between $35 and $50 an hour for productive time spent. It is not essential to attempt an accurate evaluation of a principal's time in larger organizations because measurable income is produced basically by the efforts of the staff, and the productive value of the principal's supervision is too nebulous to compute.

2. **The Charge for Employees' Time**
Time charges for the productive hours of the staff—designers, draftsmen, shoppers, job captains, etc.—is subject to specific computations.

There are approximately 235 productive days in a year, after the elimination of Saturdays, Sundays, holidays, vacations, and average sick leave. Translating productive days into hours, we find that at seven hours a day, we have 1,645 potentially productive hours per employee. This should be further reduced by deducting 5% of the time for coffee breaks and so on, leaving 1,563. If an employee earns a yearly salary of $10,000, his hourly cost is $6.40. The mark-up basis of billing time can thus lead to definite and accurately calculated charges.

155

The mark-up rate that has been arrived at in general practice by a consensus of experienced firms is that the hourly cost should be multiplied by three. The selling price for the time of the $10,000-per-year employee described in the preceding paragraph is $19.20 (three times $6.40). A chart should be prepared for each employee (or classification of employee) indicating the basic cost and billing price for each hour of each type of employees' time. The importance of such a chart in the development of residential fees should be obvious, and even more so in the determination of compensation in non-residential work.

Forms for Recording Time
In order to record time for whatever results are required—either for billing clients or for statistical information—a system should be instituted and followed. The system and its results will be only as accurate as the people who have the responsibility of recording their time. If either the principals or staff members are careless about recording time, then the results are worthless. To enable a design firm to record and assemble time information smoothly, the following forms are suggested—either to be used as they are shown here, or as a base from which to set up forms suitable to particular offices.

Exhibit A is a weekly time sheet using a code to indicate the type of work in which the staff member was engaged. The staff member (or principal) records the name of the client or clients served, the time spent, and the areas of work on a daily basis, and in addition reflects the employee's overall productivity for the week.

Exhibit B is a form accumulating the time spent on each job. The entries are made from Exhibit A by posting to the division which coincides with the code used. As the job proceeds, the designer should maintain a running total of each column, giving him a complete and up-to-date picture of where the job is going in terms of time use. The designer should note at the top of the *job time accumulation form* any information which pertains to time billing or limitations in the time allowed or the time billable for that job. At the completion of each job, all columns should be footed and the total number of hours consumed indicated. This information can then be tied in with other items of income and cost to determine the profitability of each job.

Exhibit C is one type of daily time sheet and is an excellent example of recording in detail what work has been done, and whether the time is chargeable; in addition it records expenses incurred for the job which might or might not be chargeable to the client.

Columns
1, 2, and 3—identify the client.
Column 4—indicates the *phase* of the job if the job is broken down into phases.
Column 5—describes the work done. This information is invaluable if there is a time-charge billing.
Column 6—records the number of hours spent from what hour to what hour (time should be recorded to the nearest quarter hour).
Column 7—indicates whether the time is chargeable or not.
Column 8—records expenses incurred by the designer.
Column 9—indicates whether the expenses are chargeable to the client.

Exhibit D is a Job Time Accumulation Form used in conjunction with the daily time sheet (Exhibit C). It should be noted that this form controls time right down to recording whether it has been billed

A

Weekly Time Sheet

Employee _____   Week Ending _____

Key to be used: C   — Conference   Ex-O — Expediting & Ordering
                    D-R — Designing & Rendering Es   — Estimating
                    Sh — Shopping   D   — Drafting
                    S   — Supervision

Job	Monday	Tuesday	Wednesday	Thursday	Friday	Saturday	Total
Other Time*							

* Other time is that time which cannot be charged directly to any definite job.

Form No. 14 (To obtain forms, see page 10.)

B

Job Time Accumulation

Job

Employee	Conference	Drafting	Designing and Rendering	Estimating	Shopping	Expediting and Ordering	Supervision	Other

Form No. 15 (To obtain forms, see page 10.)

C

Daily Time Sheet

Name: _____

Date: _____

Checked By: _____

Entered By: _____ Date: _____

| Form #
Job # | Client/Company | Project | Ph. | Assignment or Conference | Hours | Chg. | Expenses | | | | | |
							Travel	Amt.	Sub.	Amt.	BP	Charge to
①	②	③	④	⑤	⑥	⑦			⑧			⑨

Form No. 16 (To obtain forms, see page 10.)

D

Client Time Record						Job No.					
						Name:					
Entered By						Add:					
						Rate—Pr.		Staff			

Date	Staff	Phase	Area	Code	Detailed Explanation	Hrs.	Charge Pr.	St.	Inv. No.	Date

Form No. 17 (To obtain forms, see page 10.)

or not. If time is billable, it is entered under "Chge" PR (Principal) or ST (Staff). When the time is billed, the invoice number and date of such billing is entered in the last two columns thus effectuating complete control.

Each design firm should first analyze what information it wishes to accumulate and to what degree it wishes to control time before selecting a time-recording system. After arriving at a decision about its time requirements, it is a simple matter to devise a system based upon variations of the two sets of forms exhibited here.

Chapter Twenty-Four

Insurance

Going about his daily affairs, every businessman is constantly exposed to potential liabilities and hazards, most of which never develop. But when the unexpected catastrophe—fire, injury, robbery, etc.,—strikes, the lack of protective insurance can be a disaster. It is virtually impossible for a small business or even a large one to carry enough insurance to protect it against every possible eventuality; the cost could be prohibitive. The average businessman probably knows less about the intricacies of insurance than of any other single business element he has to contend with. It is therefore necessary to retain a reputable insurance counselor, preferably one familiar with the business problems specific to the interior design field.

The first step in the development of a sound insurance program for an interior design firm is through a discussion between the insurance counsellor, the accountant, and the principals of the firm who are most familiar with the present and future plans of the operation. This discussion should reveal all of the potential hazards to which the firm might be subject because of its activities. Obviously the scope of the suggested program will vary with the size, complexity, and needs of each particular firm, in addition to its ability to pay for insurance. The preliminary discussion should yield a list of hazard areas from which the insurance counsellor can develop the insurance needs of the firm.

After this has been done, the following information must be itemized:

1. An inventory of physical property should be produced and analyzed along the following lines:

   a. The firm's own contents on its own premises (arranged according to type, i.e., furniture and fixtures, stock for sale, decorative materials and accessories, improvements to the premises).

   b. The firm's special property (drafting equipment, blueprints and renderings, fragile objects of art, records of accounts receivable).

   c. The property of clients, or goods on consignment in the care and custody of the design firm.

2. The design firm's "floating" property must be detailed:

   a. property at exhibitions or shows
   b. property on consignment at clients' homes
   c. property being delivered to clients or being returned by them
   d. property at the premises of processors or contractors (such as upholsterers, dyers, electricians, etc.)
   e. goods imported or exported.

Once the value of these items has been determined, and their exposure to loss or damage has been estimated, the insurance counselor should prepare a detailed suggestion as to their proper protection. This suggestion will most likely include protection against loss due to fire, burglary, pilferage, water damage, breakage, losses in transit. All of these perils can be included in package policies. It is the insurance counsellor's responsibility to select the best coverage for the designer's needs. Further, it is his responsibility to point out to the insured design firm the limitations and requirements of the policies including necessary compliance with co-insurance clauses, maintenance and protective systems, and procedures to be followed in the event of a loss.

The insurance counsellor should next consider

"third party liability exposures" resulting from the firm's activities. These exposures fall into the category of bodily injury and property damage:

a. Bodily injury incurred on the premises,
b. Property damage incurred on the premises,
c. Property damage incurred off the premises,
d. Liability in connection with a product sold, specified, or installed,
e. Liability for work done under contract or any liability of others assumed in contract or purchase orders.
f. If the operation encompasses any structural alterations, specialized insurance covering the liabilities resulting from architect's errors and omissions should be considered.
g. Automobiles—any vehicle owned or regularly rented by the design firm should be properly insured. If a vehicle belonging to the principal of the firm is owned in the firm's corporate name, its insurance should be extended to include his liability arising out of the use of the automobile by an employee carrying out the business of the firm. Any vehicle leased on an occasional basis should also be insured to cover such liabilities.

Proper review of the activities of the design firm will indicate whether any of the following insurance considerations will apply:

A. Compliance with various State laws on required insurance coverage. This would include occupational injuries to employees covered under Workmen's Compensation Insurance, and non-occupational disability covered under voluntary or statutory disability benefit policies.
B. The possibility of criminal loss should be explored in detail. This includes both internal and external crime, such as infidelity on the part of employees, the pilferage of property, the theft of either payroll or cash receipts, and forgery of checks.
C. The firm's vulnerability to the loss of profits and its ability to maintain its operation in the event of fire, etc., or the possibility of extra expense through forced removal should be faced. Insurance is available to make sure that such interruptions do not force the firm out of business.
D. Where "bid or contract bonds" are required, it is essential to establish the firm's stability and performance with underwriters. A carefully studied insurance program facilitates prompt issuance of bonds when necessary.
E. The possibility of providing insurance to cover medical expenses or to compensate principals (or any other employees) against extended loss of working time through accident or illness should be reviewed.
F. A detailed study should be made of human risk factors. Depending on whether your operation is conducted as a sole proprietorship, a partnership, or a corporation, solutions should be sought to provide continuity and to avoid shrinkage or dissolution in the event of the death or disability of a principal or key person. Agreements, funded by insurance, should be drawn by your attorney to make these solutions work.
G. Profitable corporations should anticipate the retirement needs of both principals and employees, and at the same time minimize taxes, through the installation of qualified pension and/or profit-sharing plans. Partnerships and sole proprietors should explore the recently liberalized advantages of HR-10, or "Keogh" plans. The reduction of current personal income tax through deferred compensation plans, or the possibility of carrying personal insurance through "split dollar" arrangements should also be explored.

The interior designer must recognize the hazards that his *own* business may create and select from this outline the types of insurance he most needs and can afford to pay for. It is essential that the insurance program of a firm should be reviewed periodically in the light of any changes that may develop with the growth of the business. This can only be done by consulting with the insurance counsellor and making him aware of changes in the firm's circumstances and ways of conducting its affairs. Improper insurance coverage can be expensive both from a viewpoint of the cost of unnecessary coverage and the damages the firm may suffer if insurance is lacking. The selection of a competent and reliable insurance counsellor is a serious responsibility.

Chapter Twenty-Five

The Client's Job Book

Every practicing designer knows and every designer-to-be learns that interior design is a vocation in which attention to detail can never be relaxed and the recording of details can become a monumental task. It can become an all-enveloping obsession and a nightmare of gibberish, but it can also be routinized into smooth series of procedures that entail little worry and provide an immense amount of useful data, including statistical information for historical and financial analysis of the business.

Previous chapters have explained the need for the routinized sequences in the planning of a job and the estimation of a client's budget. We have illustrated routinized procedures for ordering goods and services, and controlling inventory, delivery, and billing.

Since even a modest-sized job can easily entail the planning, purchasing, expediting, and installation of more than one hundred different items of furnishing and service, it is essential to establish a cohesive assemblage of the necessary information for use during the process of the job and as a record for future reference.

This assemblage of information is the *Client's Job Book,* maintained and continuously added to from the beginning to the end of the job.

On the following pages is an almost life-size picture of a complete and actual "Client's Job Book" kept by a New York-based designer for a West Coast client. There is no need at this point to describe the forms used, how they are prepared, how they are used. All this has been fully covered in previous chapters.

The reader can easily find his way from the floor plans and its code numbers identifying specific furnishings to the Control Sheets where the ordering of these items is recorded. On these sheets each item is fully described and illustrated by samples and pictures coded to the identifying number.

Example:
On Control Sheet Page 1—*Drawing Room Page 1, Item Number 4* shown in position on the room plan of *Living Room #2* is described as: Louis XV Arm Chair, from Yale R. Burge, using two yards of cord from *Consolidated Trimming Co.* and one yard of fabric from *Clarence House, Ltd.* with the purchase order numbers and the identifying code number keyed to the plan.

If the reader will then turn to the section of this job book containing the samples and pictures, he will, under the heading "Drawing Room" find a picture identifying the Louis XV Arm Chair. The reader can then check the actual sample of the fabric to be used for this chair by referring to the page on "Fabrics—Drawing Room"; in the lower left hand corner of this page is the sample of the trimming for the same chair.

In essence, the "Client's Job Book" accumulates a complete record of all of the designer's efforts in organizing an installation. In some fashion, every interior designer must proceed through the processes of planning, scheduling purchases, gathering samples. The key to functional smoothness in this sequence of tasks is not a folder or envelope bulging with loose scribbled notes, fabric samples, wallpaper, carpeting, etc., but a compact, neat, cross-referenced work book.

Other Advantages of the Client's Job Book
1. It is immensely helpful in working with clients.

   A. Conferences with clients at any stage of the job go much more smoothly and require less of

Client's Job Book

Page 1. Control Sheet

Residence of
Room

Plan No.	Quantity	Item and No.	Firm	Ydge.	Fabric No.	Color	Firm	Finish	P.O. No.
1									
2									
3									
4	1	Louis XV arm chair 501/54	Y Burge	Cord 2 yds Fab 1 yd	# 09713 # 137195	yell+bl. yellow	CONSO Clarence H	Blue/str.yell	YB # 8801 CH # 8812

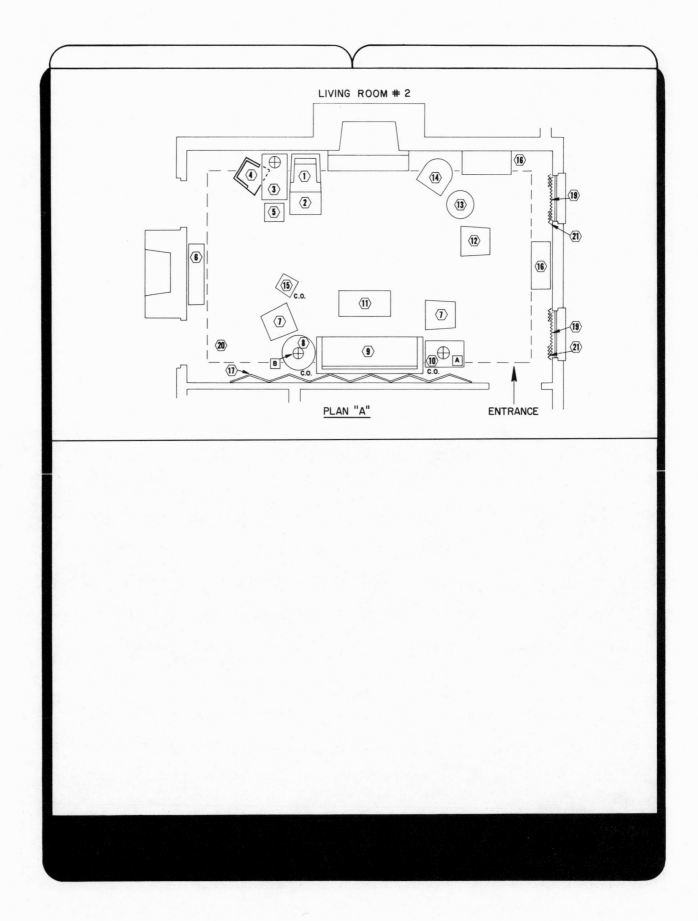

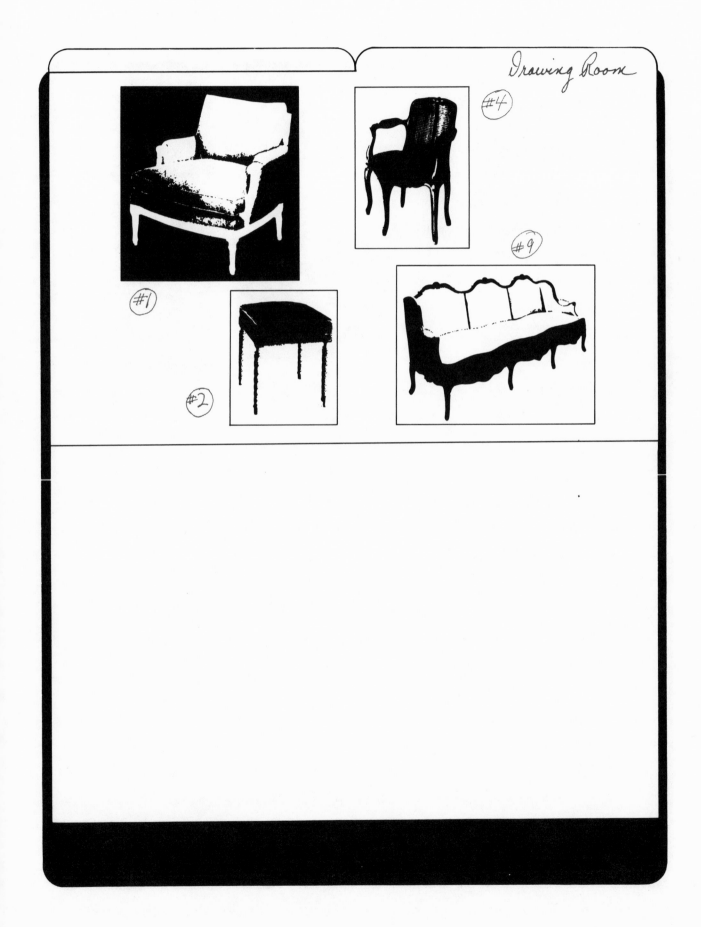

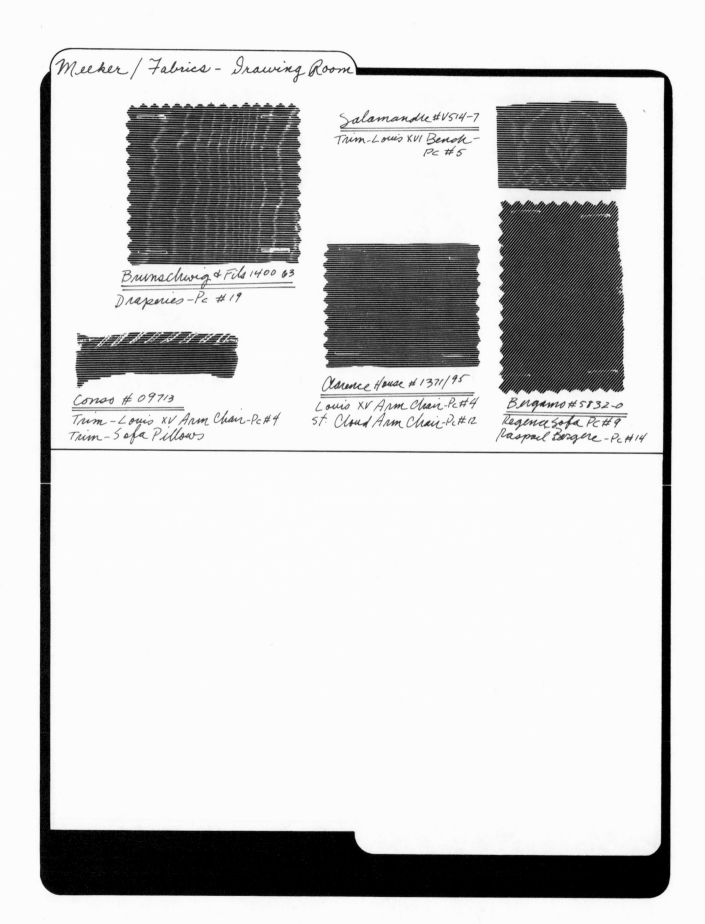

Meeker / Fabrics - Drawing Room

Brunschwig & Fils 1400 63
Draperies - Pc #19

Conso # 09713
Trim - Louis XV Arm Chair - Pc #4
Trim - Sofa Pillows

Salamandre # V514-7
Trim - Louis XVI Bench -
Pc #5

Clarence House # 1371 / 95
Louis XV Arm Chair - Pc #4
St. Cloud Arm Chair - Pc #12

Bergamo # 5832-0
Regence Sofa Pc #9
Raspail Bergere - Pc #14

the designer's time if information is readily accessible and visually presented.

B. The presentation of well-organized data can do much to enhance the designer's reputation for stability, reliability and keeping both feet on the ground.

2. It insures the availability of information to the designer and his staff.

A. The maintaining of a client's job book can only result in smooth follow-through by assistants and other members of the staff.

B. Instructions to assistants can be readily interpreted and checked.

C. In the event of the principal's absence, the work can be carried on without interruption.

D. There is no great crisis in the event that an employee leaves the firm. Almost anyone else can pick up where he left off without too much trouble.

3. It is an almost infallible record for future reference.

A. If at any time in the future the client requests changes, addition, repairs, replacements, or perhaps a new color scheme for repainting, the designer has at his fingertips a complete, easily interpreted picture of the installation.

B. In undertaking new jobs for new or old clients, the designer will find that job books on completed jobs serve as a handy guide to whatever lessons became evident as he struggled with those jobs—reminding him of points he might otherwise forget.

C. The job book, coupled with time records, cost records, and profit records, can be of invaluable assistance—

a. in determining a fee or compensation base for a new job,

b. in evaluating the advisability of continuing to work with a client or taking on new or additional jobs for the client. If the job book indicates that the client habitually makes many changes after accepting the original concept, and if the time records indicate an excessive number of hours spent on the job, the designer has a *graphic picture* of the value of that client's business.

Notes Pertaining to the Client's Job Book Illustrated Here

This job book is a fair representation of what a completed book should look like. It is a complete working record of an actual job. The book from which these pages were taken is not as complete as many in that it includes no paint schedule or cost information.

There is no paint schedule because the client's home had been painted shortly before the designer came into the picture and the paint scheme was left alone. The use and preparation of a paint schedule, however, is illustrated and described in Chapter 26 covering *"Other Forms."*

Cost information was not recorded because the system in use at this design office calls for the maintenance of all cost and income information in the bookkeeping department and not in the design department. Actually, all that would be required to complete the record would be a summary indicating the following:

Total Gross Billing	
Less : Total Price Costs	
Gross Profit	
Total Number of Hours	
Hourly Return	

Many design organizations use a more elaborate ordering control sheet, including three additional columns, as follows :

Cost of Item
Retail Price to Client
Invoice Number and Date

This gives the firm a complete financial picture in addition to providing control of the ordering process. The system used has been described in Chapter 12 with illustrated forms.

The job book illustrated can be used as a guide by any design organization, large or small, making additions or eliminations in accordance with circumstances of each particular firm.

Chapter Twenty-Six

Other Working Forms

Throughout this guide to business practices we have discussed the need for working forms, and have shown examples indicating the procedures for a successful control of the flow of paper work.

In addition to those presented in other sections of this book, there are forms designed for various specific purposes which can be adapted to the requirements of any office, and can be very helpful in controlling operations, instructions, and records. Among them are:

A. Transmittal Letters
B. Purchase Requisitions
C. Paint Schedules
D. Change Work Orders
E. Drapery Work Room Check Lists
F. Reupholstery Check Lists
G. Sales Invoices
H. Customer Credit Forms
I. Statements

A. Transmittal Letters

During the progress of a job much information is shuttled between the designer's office, the client's office, and the offices of various sources involved in the work. Needless to say, it is most important that some record be kept indicating that sketches, specifications, and other documents and instructions have been passed along. The letters of transmittal on pages 174 and 175 were designed for this function. Either can be made out by the designer in duplicate—one copy for his file, and one copy to accompany the material. The use of such forms obviates the expensive and time-consuming necessity for dictating and typing repetitive letters. Examination and study of either form indicates its simplicity, and the tremendous amount of information and control it provides with nothing more than a check mark.

It serves the additional purpose of keeping the designer alert to whatever information about the job needs to be passed along. Just looking at the form will bring key phrases and conditions to his attention.

Essentially it is a time-saver, cutting the cost of communication, and simplifying the maintenance of duplicate records for control purposes. The copy of the Transmittal Letter can be reviewed with the glance rather than with the reading and rereading of voluminous correspondence, yet it protects the designer from the uncertainties of relying on the accuracy of the spoken word.

B. The Purchase Requisition

The Purchase Order discussed in Chapter 13, represents an order placed by the designer directly with the manufacturer, supplier, or other trade source, in which case the designer assumes all liabilities attached to the placement of the order.

The *Purchase Order Requisition Form* may be substituted for the *Purchase Order Form* under two conditions:

a. When it is necessary to establish that the requirements and liabilities of the order are being assumed by someone other than the designer. The need for such clarification arises in non-residential work in connection with two distinct problems in jobs for big corporations and installations with very heavy purchasing requirements:

1. In the case of large organizations, many have purchasing departments of their own and wish to do their ordering and purchasing and to

A

Transmittal Letter

Company Name
Address

To: _____ Date: _____

_____

_____ Job: _____

Att: _____ Area: _____

We are sending you $\dfrac{\text{herewith}}{\text{under separate cover}}$ the following:

☐ Originals   ☐ Blue Prints   ☐ Photostats
☐ Samples   ☐ B & W Prints   ☐ Color Specifications
☐ Specifications   ☐ Shop Drawings

For:

☐ Estimate Only   ☐ Your Approval   ☐ Purchase Order #
☐ Your Information   ☐ Revisions   ☐ Approved as Shown

No. Copies	Dwg. #	Revised Date	Item

Copies To:

Company Name

By: _____

Form No. 18 (To obtain forms, see page 10.)

Transmittal Letter

Company Name
Address

To _____   Date _____

Address _____   Re: _____

_____   _____

_____   _____

Gentlemen: A
We are sending you the following:

☐ Prints   ☐ Shop Drawings   ☐ Herewith   ☐ By Mail
☐ Specifications   ☐ Samples   ☐ Under Separate Cover ☐ By Messenger

Drwg. No.	Latest Date	Copies Each	Description

These are sent   ☐ for approval/comments ☐ per your request   ☐ for file
                   ☐ for correction   ☐ for coordination   ☐ for information
                   ☐ for estimating   ☐ for fabrication   ☐ _____

Remarks:

_____

_____

_____

_____

If this material is not received as listed above please notify us at once

Copies to: Yours very truly,
                                     Company Name

_____

_____   by _____

Form No. 19 (To obtain forms, see page 10.)

B 1

Purchase Requisition No.

Company Name
Address _____

Source _____   Date

Address _____   Job No.

_____

Ship To _____

Address _____

_____

Client _____

_____   Area:

Mark For _____   Item No.:

Ship Via _____   When _____

Quantity	Number	Item	Color or Finish	Wood	Wholesale Per Unit	Wholesale Extended	Retail Per Unit	Retail Extended

Special instructions to be included on purchase order:

☐ For Resale
☐ Not For Resale

Company Name

Authorized By: _____

Form No. 20 (To obtain forms, see page 10.)

Requisition for Purchase Order

Client _____

Room _____

Used For _____

_____

Date _____

Due _____

Company Name
Address

Ship to _____

_____

_____

_____

B 2

To _____

_____

_____

_____

Bill to _____

_____

_____

_____

Attn: _____   Tel. _____

Quant.	Details	Unit Price	Price	Unit	Charge

Purchase Order No. _____

Confirmation _____   By: _____

177

Form No. 21 (To obtain forms, see page 10.)

maintain their own control over these functions.

2. The dollar amount of purchasing required may be so great as a) to strain the designer's credit or b) endanger the designer with tremendous liabilities. Such potential liabilities are very dangerous for small design firms. Should a problem arise in the relations of that eternal triangle of designer-client-source, the trade source will demand payment from whoever signed the purchase order. If the design firm issued its own *purchase order,* the designer would bear the liability; if the client issued the *purchase order,* the liability would be the client's.

Therefore, to allow the big corporate client the freedom of purchasing through its own organizations—and to pass the liability for purchasing to such a client, the designer should substitute a *Purchase Requisition (Form B-1)* in place of a *Purchase Order.* The requisition spells out all of the necessary details and instructions and is *sent to the client* to be transcribed onto the client's own *Purchase Order* form, signed by the client's purchasing agent, and forwarded directly by him to the trade source.

Ideally, this purchase requisition should be prepared in quadruplicate:

1. *White copy*—to the client or to whoever is doing the buying for the client,

2. *Pink copy*—to the client as a memo if the client has designated an independent buying agent,

3. *Yellow copy*—retained by the designer or job captain,

4. *Blue copy*—for the client's folder.

b. Establish a flow of information between design staff and secretarial staff.

In the larger organizations, designers must prepare purchase instructions. To expect them to sit down at the typewriter, carefully set forth all of the information, and then distribute the copies to the various departments for record control and mailing, *is a ridiculous waste of time and talent.* All that should be required is for the designer to *write out* on duplicate carbon forms all the necessary purchaing specifications and information on a *Requisition for Purchase Order (Form B-2).* One copy is sent to the typist, who then prepares the complete *Purchase Order* and distributes copies in accordance with set office routine, while the designer retains one copy for his own files.

The use of a formalized method of passing technical information along to typists can be extremely useful not only in saving time but in placing the responsibility for errors on the proper shoulders. This form takes the place of oral instructions and miscellaneous scraps of paper.

C. **Paint Schedules**

The proper application of paint colors to interior surfaces is one of the most integral phases in the achievement of the pleasant effects planned by the designer. Since the designer cannot, however, spend much of his time with painters and paper hangers (except perhaps to look over the painter's shoulder when he first mixes the paint) the instructions to the tradesmen must be devised to give concise information with minimal room for error.

Company Name
Address

Paint Schedule

Residence of

_____

_____

_____

Room	Walls		Ceiling	Wood Work			
	Walls	Paper No.		Door Trim	Windows	Ceiling Mldg.	Base Board
UPSTAIRS SITTING ROOM	Paper	P. Graf Paisley wht/blk/ red	Paint Pale ice blue as existing ceiling	Paint door casings old red as paper	Paint white as ground of paper	Paint old red as paper	Paint old red as paper
	NOTE:	(1) Paneling around fireplace breast, returns and mantel paint white as ground of paper. Cornice and base paint old red					
	NOTE:	(2) Book cabinet and new doors of book cabinet paint white as paper					
BATH adjoining New sitting Room	Paper	P. Graf "New Pais- ley Blk/wht/ red	Paper	white as paper	white as paper	None	Tile
GUEST ROOM	Paint Putty	None	off white	off wht stripe putty	off wht	Putty	Putty
	NOTE:	Board and Batten paneling alcove paint off white Base and cornice in alcove paint Putty					

SAMPLES AND PAINT DESCRIPTIONS

Off White

Putty

Old Red

Form No. 22 (To obtain forms, see page 10.)

D

Change Work Order

Company Name
Address

Date _____

Client _____

Job _____

Location _____

Description of Change or Addition _____

_____

_____

_____

_____

_____

_____

_____

_____

_____

_____

_____

_____

_____

_____

_____

_____

_____

_____

_____

Contractor's Cost _____

Signature of Contractor _____

Signature of Client's Representative _____

Signature of Job Captain _____

Form No. 23 (To obtain forms, see page 10.)

The illustrated form sets forth specific instructions and treatments for each room and for the various parts of each room. Samples of colors are attached. Wallpaper samples may be similarly attached, though the fact that wallpaper is usually delivered to the job marked for a particular client and area makes this less necessary. (This wallpaper routine should be a normal procedure, as outlined in Chapter 13 on *Purchase Orders.)*

These forms should be prepared in duplicate with:

One copy for the craftsman, and
One copy retained by the designer.

D. Change Work Order

During the process of a job which involves alterations, construction, electrical work, air-conditioning, etc., changes may arise as a result either of existing conditions or of requests by the client which necessitate changes in the original cost estimates and plans. The designer *should not* proceed with such changes unless he is specifically authorized to do so. The responsibility for incurring additional costs must be accepted by the client, otherwise the designer may leave himself open to the financial responsibility. In addition, the designer must pin down the source of additional changes made by the contractor.

When properly executed, the "change work order" will set forth the changes and establish that the client and contractor have accepted such changes and the responsibility for resulting expense.

This form should be prepared in quadruplicate:

One copy to the client,
One copy to the contractor,
One copy to the designer,
One copy to the bookkeeping department.

E. Drapery Check List

Inherent in almost every interior design installation is the production of custom-made draperies, bedspreads, and other items which require the purchase and sewing of fabrics. The vast majority of interior designers do not have their own workrooms but rely on workshops which cater to the trade. Since draperies and curtains are almost invariably custom made for each specific installation (unlike furniture and many others items which are often purchased from standard stock) the designer must establish a good working system to eliminate errors and expedite the work.

We quote the presidents of two large drapery workrooms in New York:

1. Mr. William Goldfinger, President of Continental Craftsmen, Inc. says:
"The lack of cohesive information results in a tremendous waste of the designer's time in unnecessary telephone calls and trips to the workroom. If the designer prepares his basic instructions clearly, then the workshop is in a position to assist him in setting up efficient guides to the result he has in mind."

2. Mr. William Shaffro, President of Imperial Craftsmen, Inc. says:
"The modern drapery workroom is not only equipped to handle the fabrication of draperies and curtains but to assist the designer in arriving at the technical solutions that will insure a better-than-good drapery installation and avoid costly errors and adjustments—provided that

E

Drapery Checklist

Company Name

Client _____   Date _____

Address _____

Installation Date _____

Room or Area _____

Type of Treatment: _____

_____

_____

Repeat of Fabric _____
Width of Fabric _____
Extension of Draperies _____

	Yes	No
Measure To Be Supplied by Designer		
Measure To Be Supplied by Workshop		
Wall to Wall Carpeting		
Valance Type of Valance		
Ceiling to Floor		
Ceiling to Sill		
Ceiling to Apron		
Top of Trim to Sill		
Apron		
Floor		
Unlined		
Lined		
Lined & Interlined		
Trimmed		
Stationary		
To Draw		
Tie Back		

Hardware

Type _____

_____

_____

_____

_____

_____

Work Shop Estimate $ _____

Form No. 24 (To obtain forms, see page 10.)

the designer properly prepares basic information about his design intentions."

The *Drapery Check List* is a basic outline of the information a workroom needs. The logical sequence of procedures is as follows:

The information is brought to the workroom, then reviewed and interpreted and the required services of the workroom are specified (i.e. to take measurements, make estimates, etc.). The workroom should provide the designer with:

1. A written estimate for yardage required,
2. A written estimate for labor costs,
3. A written estimate for hardware and other costs,
4. Specification of the number of widths to be used in each pair of draperies.

It is of interest to note that both **Mr. Goldfinger** and **Mr. Shaffro**, who also operate as manufacturers of custom upholstered furniture for the trade, indicate that check lists are inappropriate for upholstered furniture. Upholstered furniture is selected from stock models, and even in the interior design field there are manufacturers who will make no changes. In the case of custom upholsterers who do make changes, their procedure is to discuss such changes in detail, designating what proposals are workable and which are not. Based upon the information developed by both manufacturers, a check list on upholstery would have to be so detailed and voluminous as to be unworkable.

The recommended procedure on the development of original custom furniture or changes in standard models, is to make sketches and confer with the manufacturers.

F. **Upholstery or Reupholstery Check List**
Upholstery or reupholstery of furniture on a custom basis, when the designer is using a selected decorative fabric and a selected trade workroom, raises almost the same questions and situations as exist with custom draperies. The designer should know what he wants to do with the furniture, how it is to be upholstered or changed, rebuilt, covered or recovered. Workrooms suggest that the preparation of information as outlined in the illustrated check list, plus a conference with the workroom manager, will save the designer time and lessen the chance of errors.

G. **Sales Invoices**
Billing to clients must be handled in a fashion that will clearly indicate the facts to the client, but equally important are control for bookkeeping and reference purposes.

Prenumbered invoices should be used and such invoices should be prepared in numerical sequence in triplicate:

1. White copy for the client.
2. Yellow copy for bookkeeping purposes.
3. Pink copy for client's folder.

H. **Customer Credit Forms**
Occasionally it becomes necessary to issue a credit to a client for something previously billed. A well-coordinated system calls for credit to be designated so as to avoid confusion with *invoices*. Since credits are not issued frequently, they need not be prenumbered, but a numerical sequence should be maintained. The credit numbers can be inserted manually.

The credits should be prepared in triplicate:
1. Pink copy to the client.

183

F

Reupholstery Checklist

Company Name

Client _____   Date _____

Address _____

_____

Description of Furniture _____

_____

Style and Approximate Size _____

Repeat of Fabric _____

Width of Fabric _____

Type of Skirt _____

Type of Trim _____

Double Self Welt _____

Single Self Welt _____

Nail _____

Frame to be Tightened _____

Frame to be Touched Up _____

Change Seat Cushion   Yes ☐   No ☐

Description of Charge _____

_____

Estimate From Work Room _____

Yardage _____   Price _____

Does Price Include Pick Up & Delivery _____

Other Information _____

_____

_____

_____

_____

_____

Form No. 25 (To obtain forms, see page 10.)

Invoice

Company Name
Address

Date

Invoice No.

G

Form No. 26 (To obtain forms, see page 10.)

H

Credit

Company Name
Address

Date

Credit No.

Form No. 27 (To obtain forms, see page 10.)

Statement

Company Name
Address

I

Date			Charges	Credit	Balance	

Form No. 28 (To obtain forms, see page 10.)

2. Blue copy for bookkeeping purposes.
3. Yellow copy for the client's folder.

I. **Statements**

Once a month or more frequently, if necessary, the client should be sent a statement indicating the balance due. The statement should reflect the charges to the client and monies received or credits given during the specific billing period. The statement need only be prepared in duplicate:

1. White copy for the client.
2. Pink copy for the bookkeeping department or the client's folder.

The preceding samples of Invoices, Credits, and Statements are included to give the designer a basic format to follow. Variations in typography can be made to conform with the designer's own taste in stationery.

Chapter Twenty-Seven

Basic Elements of Bookkeeping and Accounting for the Interior Designer

It has been the writer's experience that interior designers make the worst possible candidates for the bookkeeping profession and certainly bookkeepers would probably make the worst kind of interior designer. However, it has been indicated throughout this book that certain records must be kept—not only for the proper flow of internal procedures and information, but also, and equally important, because various taxing and other governmental agencies require detailed and correct information. Therefore, the interior designer must be cognizant of the absolute need for proper accounting records.

Accounting records and systems are generally developed, installed, and maintained for functional efficiency by trained accountants. However, the amount of systematizing and degree of complexity of the records to be maintained depends upon:

1. the size of the organization
2. the volume of work to be recorded
3. the necessity to maintain absolutely correct time and cost records for fee and billing purposes
4. the firm's financial ability to pay for the time of trained staff personnel and outside accountants retained to supervise the work.

The Larger Organizations

The interior designer who is the principal or chief executive of a large design firm needs and can afford the services of either:

1. his own profesional comptroller who is an employee for the firm, and whose responsibility it is to handle all fiscal matters, install proper bookkeeping and accounting systems and to supervise all the record-keeping and/or

2. an independent Certified Public Accountant who is retained on a fee basis to work with the comptroller, or when there is no comptroller, to complete the installation of the system, supervise the activities of the bookkeeping department, analyze and interpret the financial results of the operation, and generally advise on fiscal and tax matters. In the interior design field, the accounting system need never be complex or unwieldy. A regular set of books should be maintained (with certain variations and ramifications depending upon the information required):

A. **Principal Records**
   1. Cash Receipts Journal
   2. Cash Disbursements Journal
   3. Sales Register
   4. Purchase Journal or Voucher Register
   5. Petty Cash Journal
   6. Accounts Receivable Ledger
   7. Accounts Payable Ledger
   8. General Ledger
   9. General Journal

The use of these journals is fairly standardized in the business world and the only comment necessary concerns the Sales Register and Purchase Journal.

The Sales Register should record and analyze each sales invoice prepared, indicating sufficient information for sales tax purposes and division of income. Exhibit A is a basic format and can be further developed with additional columns indicating, for example, a further breakdown of the application of sales tax ((or non-sales tax) information (depending upon the geographical taxing locality and the omission of sales tax from sales of particular services).

If the designer sells his own inventory, a column can be set up in the sales register which would indi-

A

		Date	Clients Name	Inv. #	Acct. Rec.	Sales		Fees		Time Charges	Other Income	Sales Tax	Delivery Charges	Sales from Invent.
						1	2	3	4	5	6	7	8	9	10
						Res	Non Res	Res	Non Res					
1														
2														
3														
4														
5														
6														
7														
8														
9														
10														
11														
12		Res - Residential				Non Res - Non Residential								

Sales Register

cate such sales and accumulate the necessary information to compare the percentage of income as profit from the sale with the other kinds of income realized by the sale. It is almost axiomatic that while in many other businesses a complete sales register is not maintained because of the amount of work entailed, in the interior design field it is a must because of the very important control information it yields.

The Purchase Journal (Exhibit B) is the other register which needs amplification in that it should be broken down sufficiently to record the auxiliary information documented in the sales register:

Purchases for residential clients
Purchases for non-residential clients
Job Costs—These columns accumulate cost information which may or may not be billable to the client but affect the gross profit of each job.

This chapter cannot possibly set forth a complete set of records or chart of accounts as a standard guide for the profession. A set of standard account books and charts of accounts breakdowns would be inappropriate for the larger firm, since the detailed records kept and the depth of systematic analysis based upon them would depend completely upon the size, functions, and needs of each particular firm. Variations from what accountants would consider standard account books could be set up only by trained accountants or management consultants with a knowledge of the interior design field—or simply through trial and error experience. Our illustration indicates, however, that with proper records a design firm can obtain such information about its own operation as the Analysis of Income Sources (page 193) indicating sources of income and direct costs of design.

This type of analysis, when carried out and corre-

lated to other expense factors involved in each segment of the income source (as in comparing the cost of time with the income earned in that same time) can give management an excellent guide to the profitable operation of the business.

Work in Process
An important factor involved in proper accounting techniques is the financial effect of "work" or jobs in process" at the time any particular statement is rendered. *Work in process* is best described as those items of furnishing or service for which a designer has been billed by a trade source and which he has not yet billed to the client. To overlook this factor is to arrive at incorrect statement figures.

If the accounting system is set up properly, the *work in process* is arrived at quite simply. A perfect example can be seen in the *client's inventory sheet* described in Chapter 14. Reference to this chapter will indicate that the receipt of the source's invoice is noted on the form by a red check mark where the item is listed. Until the item is billed to the client, it is an open item of inventory.*

*Note: This is true only if the vendor's invoice has been paid or entered in the *accounts payable control* (if one is maintained).

The Small or One-Man Firm
The interior designer whose firm is a small or "one-man" type of operation will very often find that he is unable to afford not only a comptroller but a full-time bookkeeper and even if he can afford a qualified bookkeeper, he hasn't enough work to justify hiring one. He can get by adequately with a part-time bookkeeper and/or a periodic visit from an accountant. If he does, however, it is necessary for him to devote some of his precious time to maintaining a simple set of basic records so that:

1. He will have enough information readily avail-

B

	Date	Vendor	acct. Payable	Client Purchase			Job Costs			Other Purchases	
				Res	non Res	Inv	Client Charge	Non Charge			
				1	2	3	4	5	6	7	8	9	10
1											
2											
3											
4											
5											
6											
7											
8											
9											
10											
11											
12											

Purchase Journal

Analysis of Income Sources

Commercial Fees				
Royalties			600	
Commissions			7200	
Contract Services			10800	
Time changes			4300	
Total Commercial Fees				22900
Residential Fees				
Commissions			13700	
Contract Services			15900	
Time			20100	
Total Residential Fees				49700
Decorating				
Sales - Commercial		16600		
Sales - Residential		362000		
			378600	
Cost of Sales				
Inventory - beginning		63000		
Purchases - Commercial		10600		
Purchases - Residential		230000		
Purchases - Stock		3200		
Freight and Delivery		500		
		307300		
Less: Inventory at End		19000		
Cost of Sales			288300	
Decorating Income				90300

C

able at all times, in simple form, to guide and control his everyday financial activities, such as his transactions with clients and trade sources.

2. Information will be easily available in concise and useable form for either a part-time book-keeper, or for the accountant, who may come in periodically and/or at the end of the year, to pick up the information they need.

3. There will be a base from which to construct tax information and enough financial information to afford the designer some interpretation of his activities.

By giving a little time to record keeping, and by being orderly and neat, the designer can actually reduce his expenses and more important, know what he is doing at all times. Without some semblance of order, the mass of papers that must be handled is enough to create a limitless confusion.

The small design firm must:
1. Maintain records to control the flow of the work in progress.
2. Maintain a record of funds received and funds disbursed.
3. Maintain a record to control sales and record the sales taxes due to the taxing authorities.
4. Maintain a record of financial transactions with trade sources.
5. Maintain a record of the clients' financial transactions.

The following exhibits and illustrations will indicate to the reader that it is relatively simple and easy to maintain records without being a trained bookkeeper:

1. **Design Work-Flow Records**

The records for controlling work flow have been thoroughly discussed in prior chapters and from the material presented, the designer should be able to develop a system with which he can work easily.

2. **Funds Received and Funds Disbursed**
   A. **Funds Received—Exhibit C**
   All monies received by the designer from every source and deposited in his checking account must be listed in a cash receipts book and entered in the appropriate column.

   B. **Funds Disbursed—Exhibit D**
   A record of every check issued by the designer is made on this record and entered in the appropriate column.

3. **Record of Sales and Sales Taxes—Exhibit E**
   Every invoice prepared by the designer to be issued to his client is entered in numerical sequence and analyzed in the appropriate columns.

4. **Control of Transactions with Trade Sources— Exhibit F**
   One of the most annoying problems that the small design firm must face is that of controlling payments to sources and suppliers. Errors can be made in payments, invoices may be paid twice, credit for deposits given may not be taken, and so on. The use of the purchase control is an effective method of coping with such problems.

5. **Transactions with Clients—Exhibit G**
   The designer should always maintain a separate account for each client indicating the monies received and the invoice rendered. Maintaining this ledger account will always indicate quickly what balance a client owes him.

	Date	Received From	Amount	Balance Due from Client	Deposit from Client			Other Item	Amount
			1	2	3	4	5	6	7	8	9	10
1	Mar 1	John Jones	2000-					Capital	2000-
2	Mar 5	Elaine Brown	500-		500-				
3	Mar 15	Elaine Brown	585-		585-				
4	Mar 25	Elaine Brown	89.40	89.40					
5									
6									
7			3174.40	89.40	1085-				2000-
8									
9									
10									
11									
12									

Cash Receipts   Month of ——— 196—

D

	Date	To Whom Paid	Ck #	Amount	Purchases For Client	amount	stock	Personal Drawing	Petty Cash	Other Item	amt.
				1	3	5	6	7	8	9	10
1	Mar 4	ABC Stationers	101	72 40						Stationery	72 40
2	4	Frank Smith	102	150 —						Legal	150 —
3	15	Alan Furn. Co.	103	300 —	Brown – Deposit	300					
4	15	Gerald Fab. Co	104	50 —	ˮ ˮ	50					
5	21	John Jones	105	75.20				60 —	15.20		
6	21	Carol Antique Shop	106	100 —			100				
7	26	Gerald Fab. Co.	107	60 —	Brown Balance	60					
8											
9				807.60		410 —	100 —	60 —	15.20		222 40
10											
11											
12											

Cash Disbursements   Month of ———— 196—

E

				1	2	3	4	5	6	7	8	9	10
				Sales month of ——— 196—									
		Name	Inv #	Amount		Sales Txble.	Non Txble	Sales Tax	Freight	Fees		Other Item	Amt.
1	Mar 22	Elaine Brown	101	174.40		170—		3.40	1—				
2	26	Elaine Brown	102	1,060.50		1000—		20—	40.50				
3													
4				1,234.90		1170—		23.40	41.50				
5													
6													
7													
8													
9													
10													
11													
12													

F

Vendor's Control		Month of						196	
		1	2	3	4	5	6	7	8	9	10
Date	Vendor	amount of Invoice	Paid Date	Check #		Deposits with Vendor Date	Amt.	Vendor offset	Date	Billed to Client Inv.#	amt.
1 Mar 15	Alan Furniture Co.					3/15	300-				
2 15	Gerald Fabrics Co.					3/15	50-	3/26 (a)			
3 21	Gerald Fabrics Co.	110 -	3/26	#107 (a)					3/22	101	170-
4 26	Alan Furniture Co.	600 -		(B)					3/26	102	1000-
5 27	Vita Trucking Co.	40.50							3/26	102	40.50
6									note C		

Note (a) Deposit of $50 to Gerald Fabrics Co. is coupled with payment for the balance to indicate that the vendor's invoice is fully paid.

Note (b) Alan Furniture Co. invoice of $600 is open and unpaid but there is a deposit of $300 which has not been offset – leaving a balance of $300

Note (c) This record of Vendor's Control can be used as a control for billing purposes.

Sheet No.					Account No.			
Terms					Name *Client Account — Elaine Brown*			
Rating					Address			
Credit Limit								
Date 19........	Items Charged to Client	Folio	✓	Debits	Date 19........	Items Received from Client	Folio	✓	Credits
Mar. 22	Inv. #101		a	174.40	Mar 5	Retainer — apply to Final Bal			500-
26	Inv. #102			1065.50	15	Confirmation Deposit $585			
						Sofa & Chair			500-
						Fabric		a	85-
					25	Payment		a.	89.40

Note (a) Since the client paid the invoice for the fabric first
with a deposit of 85⁰⁰ and then a payment for the balance
the transaction is complete and the items are lettered off (a) to
indicate no balance for that particular invoice.

The next time completely paid will be lettered off (b), the next (c) and
so on.

In order to understand the use of the recorded memoranda shown in the various forms used as exhibits in this chapter as well as the information derived from them, examples of transactions will be set forth and posted to the exhibited forms.

A. March 1—Designer John Jones deposits $2,000 as initial working capital—(entered Cash Receipts Journal, Exhibit C, line 1)

B. March 4—Pays for stationery by check $72.40 (entered Cash Disbursements, Exhibit D, line 1). Pays attorney fee $150 (Exhibit D, line 2)

C. March 5—Signs contract with new client Elaine Brown and receives $500 retainer:
   (a. Enter in Exhibit C, Cash Receipts Journal
   (b. Open ledger account for client Elaine Brown, Exhibit G and enter receipt of money from her.)

D. March 15—Client Elaine Brown signs a confirmation to purchase the following items and gives the designer a 50% deposit of $585.

Sofa	$ 600.
Club Chair	$ 400.
17 yards of fabric	$ 170.
	$1,170.

(Enter Receipt of Cash in Exhibit C; Enter in Ledger Account for Elaine Brown)

E. March 15—Designer places the orders for this merchandise and is required to give deposits to the vendors. Designer gives the following checks, (enter in Exhibit D and Exhibit F):

Alan Furniture Co.	$300.
Gerald Fabric Co.	$50.

F. March 21—Designer draws check for $75.20; for personal use $60 and reimbursement of expenses $15.20. (Enter in Exhibit D).

G. March 21—Designer buys an antique lamp from Carol Antiques for inventory $100. (Enter in Exhibit D).

H. March 21—Receives invoice from Gerald Fabric Co., March 28—$110. (Enter in first column only Vendors Control—Exhibit F).

I. March 22—Invoices client Elaine Brown for fabric—

Fabric	$170.00
Sales Tax 2%	3.40
Delivery Charge	1.00
	$174.40
Less paid on A/C (Confirmation #1)	85.00
	$ 89.40

(Enter in Sales Journal, Exhibit E and Client Account for Exhibit G).

J. March 25—Client Elaine Brown pays invoice for fabric in sum of $89.40. (Enter in Exhibit C—Cash Receipts; Enter in Elaine Brown Ledger Sheet.)

K. March 26—Designer pays Gerald Fabric Co. balance due of $60. (Enter in Exhibit D—Cash Disbursements; Enter payment in Vendors Control Exhibit F indicating date of payment.)

L. March 26—Receives invoice from Alan Furniture Co. for sofa and chair $600. (Enter in Vendors Control—Exhibit F)

M. March 26—Billed Client Elaine Brown

Sofa	$ 600.00
Chair	400.00
	$1,000.00
2% Sales Tax	20.00
	$1,020.00
Freight	40.50
	$1,060.50
Less deposit	500.00
	$ 560.50

(Enter in Sales Journal—Exhibit E and Client Ledger Account—Exhibit G)

N. March 27—Receives invoice from Vita Trucking Co. for above $40.50. (Enter in Vendors Control Exhibit F)

At this point if the reader will review the entries made and the results reflected in the books, he will find:

Exhibit C—Deposited	$3,174.50
From the following sources:	
Investment	$2,000.00
Received from client	1,174.50

Exhibit D—Disbursed for month	$807.60
For:	
Payments for Client's goods	$410.00
Purchased Inventory	100.00
Personal Use	60.00
Petty Cash	15.20
Stationery	72.40
Legal	150.00

Exhibit E—Sales for the month	$1,234.90
Of which Taxable Sales are	$1,170.00
Due for Sales Taxes	23.40
Reimbursement for delivery charges	41.50

Exhibit F—	
Indicates balance due to	
Alan Furniture Co.	$300.00
Invoice $600 less open deposit of $300	
Invoice due to Vita Trucking Co.	40.50

This exhibit also indicates that all goods and services purchased for clients have been billed out. (This is another method for Inventory Control.)

Exhibit G—
Client Account for Elaine Brown:
Invoice #101 has been paid in full.

Invoice #102 for $1,060.50 is unpaid except there is a deposit of $500., leaving a balance of $560.50 to be collected and in addition the designer has a $500 retainer which can be applied against the account at any time.

The Daily Diary

The designer's daily diary is another simple recording device which plays an important and necessary role in accumulating information. Essentially it should be used in order to accomplish the following two purposes:

1. To record time, not only to direct the activities of the designer in respect to the allocation of his day but to record time spent with a client.

2. To record out-of-pocket business expenses for which the designer should reimburse himself

since they are valid deductions for tax purposes. At the present time the tax department
requires that a record of expenses be maintained indicating—*when, where, why* and *with
whom* the expenditure is made. The diary is
now an acceptable record to the Internal Reve-
nue Service if maintained properly.

The diary should record in the following manner:

Monday—March 4   11:00 AM to client Elaine
                  Brown's taxi $1.80
                  3:00 PM return to office
                  taxi $2.00

Tuesday—March 5   With client Elaine Brown
                  at Gerald Fabric Co.
                  showroom 11:00 AM to
                  11:45 AM. Lunch with
                  Elaine Brown at Pablo's $9.40
                  With client Elaine Brown at
                  Alan Furniture Co. showroom
                  1:30 PM to 2:30 PM
                  Taxis from Pablo's to
                  showrooms and return to
                  office $4.20

If the diary is maintained as indicated, the designer can cull time information from it to record
on time accumulation records. He is also able to
reconstruct his expenses for reimbursement and to
show a permanent back-up record for tax purposes.

Edited by Olga Gueft, Editor of INTERIORS
Design Director, Anthony Aviles
Design and Typography by Harper & George
Printed and bound by Halliday Lithograph Corp.